vile france

vile france
Fear, Duplicity, Cowardice and Cheese

Denis Boyles

ENCOUNTER BOOKS
SAN FRANCISCO

First edition published in 2005 by Encounter Books, an activity of Encounter for Culture and Education, Inc., a nonprofit corporation.

Encounter Books website address: www.encounterbooks.com

Manufactured in the United States and printed on acid-free paper.

The paper used in this publication meets the minimum requirements of ANSI/NISO Z39.48-1992 (R 1997)(*Permanence of Paper*).

FIRST EDITION

Library of Congress Cataloging-in-Publication Data

Boyles, Denis.
    Vile France : fear, duplicity, cowardice and cheese / Denis Boyles.
      p. cm.
    Includes index.
    ISBN 1-59403-052-9 (alk. paper)
    1. Anti-Americanism—France. 2. France—Relations—United States. 3. United States—Relations—France. 4. France—Politics and government. I. Title.
    DC417 .B6 2005
    944.083—dc22

                                       2005042036

10 9 8 7 6 5 4 3 2 1

Dedicated to Marcel Marceau

contents

preface

France does not know it, but we are at war with America. Yes, a permanent war, a vital war, a war without death. Yes, they are very hard the Americans, they are voracious, they want undivided power over the world.
—former French president François Mitterrand, quoted by George-Marc Benamou

IT'S HARD TO GET EXCITED about a mostly nonviolent war with an incidental nation like France. I mean, there are no French battleships in Boston harbor. In fact, there are no French battleships anywhere. And the idea of French marines landing on Coney Island doesn't quite excite the fear mechanism of most Americans.

What Mitterrand meant was that while the French people don't know it, the French government is at war with the United States—and has been, as Mitterrand said, more or less permanently for the last two centuries. The France that Mitterrand was talking about is the nation that's an ongoing invention of its snooty, elitist, self-satisfied, self-obsessed, humorless, Paris-dwelling governing class. Schooled and trained apart from the people it rules, inculcated with a belief in chauvinistic superiority, this ruling class seeks to perpetuate and further its own causes, many of which have nothing at all to do with the welfare of the French people.*

---

*This notion does only minimal damage to the general thesis of political historian Pierre Rosanvallon's Le Modèle politique français, an insightful condemnation of France's caricature of democracy.

The governments of France, past and present, exist to give these elites power, money and influence. French governments have never been overly concerned with égalité, let alone liberté. Even their affection for fraternité stops at the outer limits of rhetoric and theory. The twin goals of the government of France are to keep the people of France out of the streets of Paris, which is where almost all meaningful political reform takes place in France, and to keep the political class rolling in loot and reclining in comfort.

That doesn't leave a lot of time for thinking, so ever since the French Revolution, the principal intellectual preoccupation of France's ruling class has been to precisely define France in apophatic terms—as what it is not. And these days what France is not, as every Frenchman agrees, is America. Consequently, anti-Americanism is woven through the entire concept of the state and, to the extent possible by official means, through the culture as well. To remove it would be to unravel all that has been built over the last two hundred years, and especially since the end of World War II. If France were not anti-American it simply would not be France. That is the France that is so despicable and the France that is at war with us.

The other France, the geographical one where all those charming French people live, is overtaxed and over-regulated and worried about its future. The French people aren't at war with any-one, except perhaps their own government. While the government of France betrays its ostensible allies by aiding their enemies, the French people wage war the best way they know how: by cheating on their taxes and complaining about everyone else.

And they are ferocious complainers. They complain about us, about Algerians and Moroccans, about Jews, about work (a lot), about other Europeans, about the Church. They give the elites almost two-thirds of whatever they make, and spend their working lives in dead-end jobs producing practically nothing, if current labor figures are right. In return, they are given subsidized food and subsidized newspapers, state-run utilities, state-run trains, cheap wine and profoundly dull television programming. Robbed of initiative and drugged by benefits, the French are largely content to watch as France staggers along on its slow meander toward bankruptcy in several flavors and an eventual purgatory as an Islamic republic.

The French never tire of pointing out the discrepancy between the governed and the government of the United States: "It's not you I dislike, monsieur," said nearly every French person with whom I've spoken since 9/11. "It's your government." Generally, this little speech is followed by a pause into which I am expected to deposit my own self-loathing agreement.

But it's not the French I dislike, messieurs. It's France. It is impossible to overstate the wickedness of the French elites, starting with the first drop of the guillotine's blade in 1789 and up to and including their complicity in undermining the Security Council and their sharing in the corruption of the United Nations— and especially in the recent Oil-for-Food scandal. The people who run the place are corrupt in every possible meaning of the word. They disgrace the simple elegance of the nation's 60 million charming inmates.

■ ■ ■ ■ ■

A PERSONAL EXAMPLE: Several years ago, when my family and I first decided to start spending more time each year in Europe, we chose a rural part of France, for the simple reason that some friends of ours own a large, beautiful and often unoccupied farmhouse there. The Sunday after we first arrived, the local schoolmaster stopped by to say hello, followed by a retired farmer. The next day, our car broke down, leaving us with three small children, two bicycles and an empty kitchen. My wife decided to pedal the six kilometers into town to visit the grocery while I set up a temporary office and tried to get some work done. The children, bored, asked what they could do. It was a beautiful, sunny afternoon. I pointed to a large, green iron crucifix at a crossroads. "Why not see where the road on the right leads?" Off they went, and off I went to work.

It didn't seem like it had been three hours since my wife had left, but I looked up and there she was, flushed and unsuccessful in her search for food—it was early-closing day in the town and nothing was open. "Where are the children?" she asked mildly.

What an excellent question to put to such an incompetent father. I explained what I had done on my way out the door.

By this time, it was late in the afternoon. On bicycles we crisscrossed farm lanes and rural roads asking everyone we passed if they had seen our missing children, who knew very little French and didn't know the address of the farmhouse. It was getting dark. Finally, a woman working in her garden listened to my hurried inquiry, then said simply, "But, monsieur, this is a serious matter. You must inform the gendarmes."

So I did. Returning to the farmhouse, I called the cops. A neighbor came by to ask what was going on. She had received a telephone call from somebody saying the children were missing. She put my wife in her car and they set off. The schoolmaster came by, heard the story, and set off in another direction. The gendarmes showed up—three of them, an obviously superior, older officer and two young underlings. The officer explained that a helicopter was en route, along with a detachment of bloodhounds. All this within minutes.

I told the police that I had thought the children would just go look a few hundred yards down the road, then come back and tell me that the road led into the French countryside or to a farm or something. I didn't get one single bad-dad glance (I know them when I see them), and nobody lectured me on the literal-mindedness of children. I explained that I had no idea they would do exactly as I had told them for perhaps the only time in their lives. This is Europe, I thought to myself; that road, in theory, leads to China.

The gendarmes were collecting photographs of the children when the schoolmaster pulled up with the kids in the car. "They remembered me from last night," he said, happily.

As the gendarmes called off the chopper and the dogs, their captain, a man with a broad smile and rich embroidery on his kepi, kept brushing off my apologies. "It's a beautiful day. I love to get out of the office, monsieur," he said, smiling. "And this is the way these stories are supposed to end."

Fifteen minutes later, a small crowd comprising virtually all the people with whom we had spoken on our desperate little search showed up at the kitchen door. The schoolmaster greeted them and explained what had happened. Everyone waved and smiled. The children waved back. We offered coffee on a bluff, since there was none in the house. My wife looked at me with something approaching pity, but that may have been thinly veiled disgust. I smiled at the children. The children smiled at the schoolmaster. Then everyone broke into smiles, laughed those little French laughs—say "ho, ho" through your nose and you're there—clapped each other on the back, and went home again. It was a little Pagnol moment.

I later found out they all thought I was British.

■ ■ ■ ■ ■

LOVING THE FRENCH but hating France is very much like loving the sinner but hating the sin. Yes, there's an obvious and direct connection between the state and its citizens, even in France. And there are always stories about Americans being berated and spat upon in Paris. But there are also two Frances. One is wretched. And despite the fact that I use the word indiscriminately in this essay, the other is not.

This little book is about the wretched ones—those who govern France, who encourage anti-Americanism, who trade with corrupt and murderous states and who are profoundly corrupt themselves, who support genocide and terrorism, so long as it isn't on their doorstep, and who have created a failing state for all those other Frenchmen, about whom their knowledge is only anecdotal, but who are treated with cynical contempt by their rulers, even as they manipulate them along the road to financial, political and cultural ruin.

AN EXCULPATORY NOTE: This book, as the publisher has happily made clear, is a polemic—which is more truth-in-packaging than you'll find in Le Monde and the rest of the French press. A French journalist asked me once why I lived outside the Île-de-France "with the stupid farmers." He didn't know the area at all. "Can they read? Or do they just watch the television?" No wonder the French national press is one of the most undercirculated in Europe. The French who live beyond the Parisian Pale, the French who live farthest figuratively and literally from the ruling class, the French who live around the edges of the hexagon that describes France, are extraordinarily charming, polite and helpful if often misguided people.

As I'm certain they would agree, it's what happens down at the other end of the autoroute that makes France repugnant, and that's the focus here.

■ ■ ■ ■ ■

MUCH OF THIS was written while I was observing the European press for National Review Online, and some portion of this book appeared there in different form. I'm grateful to Kathryn Jean Lopez for her perhaps unwitting complicity in this project.

I also hired a young researcher to help with the writing of this book, but she kept disappearing to deal with incomprehensible romantic and other personal issues. Any errors in these pages are hers.

—Denis Boyles

the war

HERE'S WHAT WE AMERICANS KNOW for sure about France: it's the annoying but well-dressed country where Brigitte Bardot lives and where all the men talk like Charles Boyer. In France, they smoke cigarettes that smell like sweat-sock emulsion. They are arrogant and they love women and wine and cheese and all that. Most of us are irritated by whatever it was they did to us at the United Nations before the war in Iraq, but most of us weren't really paying attention. We do know that we saved their country a couple of times, because we've seen movies about it.

So, Francewise, our understanding is a little thin. In fact, our most enduring myth about France is that French guys know nothing about war but all about love, especially when zay speak Fwench, zee language of womance. No wonder the most impressive Frenchman to most Americans is Pepé Le Pew, the self-proclaimed "locksmith of love" who has found work in this country as a cartoon skunk at Warner Brothers. He's an inspiration to his countrymen, too: When an expat Frenchman decided to throw a series of parties mostly to help other Frenchmen in New York score with "very liberated" American women, he posted an online invitation reading, "You have a particular taste for red wine, cheese, smokers, you like bubbles, play *pétanque*....You have already qualified to join our happy, trendy, hip ... parties." Of course, advertising for women who like bubbles, *pétanque* and trendy parties is a no-fail way to flush a reporter from the *New Yorker.* As the *maître de cool* explained to her, "We French have the image of being arrogant

1

and loving women and wine and cheese and all that. And, you know, it's true, we are that way!" We know!

In fact, the French do know how to wage a war. It's not how we do it, but it works for them. After two centuries of elitist-inspired Yank-bashing, an intense, obvious, mindless dislike of America burns in the heart of most Parisians and virtually every French political figure. As a rule, it's kept well hidden behind the sardonic insincerity that produces gaseous phrases like "your oldest friend"—the kind of sentiment that the French dispense so we don't backhand them into bankruptcy. French "friendship" is the sort of effervescence that Americans, always suckers to be admired as nice guys, swallow eagerly. But occasionally, the truth slips out, as demonstrated by the infamous remark of Mitterrand that begins this book.

At the time he made it, America, along with the rest of the world, laughed it off. France? Our old ally from the days of Lafayette? But we should have taken Mitterrand at his word, because he not only meant it, he was restating a fact that has been clear to every French ruler since Napoleon. France has always been at war with America, but we're only now beginning to notice it. President George W. Bush has furrowed his brow and mangled many simple sentences during his extended presidency, but none so badly as when, on the sixtieth anniversary of the D-Day landings, he went to Normandy stood next to Jacques Chirac and said that if called on to do so, America would gladly send boys off to die for France yet again—when what he probably meant to say was that he would reform Social Security right after the next election.

America may deserve George W. Bush. In a democracy, as Mencken said, you get what you deserve, "good and hard." But America doesn't deserve French enmity. And when it comes to France, President Bush and his successors will have to see the anti-American policy of the French government for what it is: the long-term work of a "soft" enemy (as opposed to "hard" ones, like all those nasty North Koreans) whose influence will grow like a big,

2

toxic *champignon*, especially if the European Union becomes the "counterweight" to the United States that France desperately longs and needs for it to be. As European policy analyst John C. Hulsman said in a recent Heritage Lecture, "We need to stop thinking that French rhetoric isn't serious, that it's just a cultural eccentricity.... [I]t reflects the honest beliefs of a people that have a very different political and economic agenda from ours."

In very large numbers, the French don't like us. According to recent polls, fewer than 5 percent of them admitted to harboring *any* admiration for the United States. What we mistakenly see as a craven, anti-Semitic, insecure, hypocritical, hysterically anti-American, selfish, overtaxed, culturally exhausted country, bereft of ideas, fearful of its own capitulation to Islam, headed for a demographic cul de sac, corrupted by lame ideologies, clinging to unsupportable entitlements, crippled by a spirit-stomping social elite and up to its neck in a cheesy soufflé of multilayered bureaucracy is actually worse than all that. It's *vile*.

In just the last half-century or so, France has been guilty of eagerly abetting the Holocaust; perpetrating more postwar anti-Semitic acts than any other country in Europe; enabling and supporting state-sponsored genocide and slaughter in Africa and Asia; attacking unarmed civilians on foreign territory; arming enemies of Western democracies; treating its young with disdain and its elderly with a neglect that is often fatal; suppressing conventional human rights, especially the right to free speech; protecting murderers and war criminals from justice; pursuing a foreign policy in which mendacity is a strategy used against both friends and enemies; polluting the earth while rhetorically demanding planetary hygiene from others; pursuing illegal trade activities; engaging in massive, systemic corruption and greed; worshipping self-seriousness; and undermining American foreign policy whenever possible, no matter how many lives that costs. France looks great and seems swell, but it acts hideously. It's the Ted Bundy of European nations.

The more belligerent France's behavior toward the United States becomes, the more often you hear palliative nonsense, like this remark by the president of the French-American Chamber of Commerce: "We must remember that for more than two centuries, France and America have never been enemies but rather allies; they have never fought a war against one another but rather have fought together against common enemies."

Here's a list of common enemies that France and the United States have fought together in two-hundred-odd years of declared wars:

■ Germany

1.

It is true that America has never bothered to go to war with France. That is not to say that France has not gone to war with America. When we were a British colony, France was our last enemy. When America became independent, France was our first enemy. When America went to war in Iraq, France was our most persistent enemy. In every conflict in between, save possibly the First World War, France has been on the wrong side of us, and therefore on the wrong side of history. France's constant tactic has always been deceit punctuated by fits of surrender, especially to Germans and more recently to Islamic terrorists in Palestine and elsewhere.

"A 200-year-old friendship ..."; "... The strong ties that bind France and the U.S. [in] an alliance over two centuries old ..."; "... a 225-year-old alliance"—blurbs of this kind are on practically every book about the French-American relationship. If you Google "France America alliance" (admittedly, a lousy way to Google), you'll get over two million results.

It's all a myth. The reality is not exactly a secret history— most of the incidents that describe the relationship between the two countries are taught in schools. But they are rarely presented in a way to help a student realize that France and America are bound not by mutual admiration, but by 225 years of French animosity and betrayal, fecklessness and fear.* An average historian could easily find examples of French animosity at work every second of every day during that time, because when it comes to condescension and irritation toward America, France is a habitual offender.

■ ■ ■ ■ ■

DURING THE COLONIAL PERIOD, French scientific experts were claiming that only inferior breeds of dogs, horses and humans could possibly be grown in America—something about the air. While German, British, Irish, Scandinavian, Spanish and Portuguese immigrants were swapping the limitations of one hemisphere for the limitless possibilities of another, the French were staying home. When they did venture abroad—into one of their African or Southeast Asian colonies, for example—they insisted that they were *still* at home. Trying to convince people like the Algerians that they were really French never did work.

During the American Revolution, Lafayette defied the wishes of the French government by coming to America, and managed to get a significant number of French troops on the ground only by convincing his government that the Americans were enemies of their enemy, not friends of France. The pre-revolutionary monarchy of France had little interest in being an accomplice to an antimonarchist revolution.

---

*The long history of French-American animosity is something of interest on both sides. In France, Philippe Roger's *L'Ennemi américain* provides a very detailed checklist of American offenses based on stereotypes that have been carefully nurtured over the centuries and that resemble a variant of racism more than just a simple antipathy. The book was a bestseller in France. In the U.S., I'm sure John J. Miller and Mark Molesky's *Our Oldest Enemy* similarly explodes the myth of Franco-American amity, although I have not yet seen that book. The authors maintain a Web site at www. oldestenemy.com.

But immediately after the American Revolution, and after watching the new but impoverished nation sell off its navy and disband its army, the French waged an undeclared war on the largely defenseless Americans. In the first six months of 1797 alone, more than three hundred American ships were seized by France in an effort to stop British-American trade, part of America's determined neutrality in the wars that the Europeans fought with each other.

It was an independent America's first war, a perfect precursor of what would become the model for conflict with the French— a war undeclared, but waged with a kind of feline ferocity in which the enemy defaults to acquiescent sullenness when cornered. Eventually, that first campaign—the "Quasi War," as historians call it— resulted in a national mobilization against a French invasion that was thought to be imminent. Alexander Hamilton was detailed to organize a standing army for George Washington, who came out of retirement and rode into the capital to answer President John Adams' call to lead the Americans into battle. Meanwhile, the United States quickly moved to refloat a navy capable of defending the nation's interests against France. The USS *Constellation* and the USS *Constitution*—the famed "Old Ironsides"—both saw their first action in battle against the French. All this took place against the resolute hostility of Vice President Thomas Jefferson and his Republicans, whose steadfast defense of the French more or less mirrors the Francophilia of today's Democrats. When the bloody excesses of the French Revolution collapsed into what popular historian Thomas Fleming called "an orgy of mob rule and raw terror" so great that Americans fled the country, Jefferson shrugged it off, saying that the French cause was worth having "half the earth desolated." In this regard, Stalin was a Jeffersonian democrat.

America's first war against the French was not without colorful incidents, either: In one stirring adventure straight out of *Hornblower*, the captain of the *Constitution* cornered a notorious

French corvette, a captured British ship called the *Sandwich*, in the harbor of Porto Plata in what is now the Dominican Republic. The ship had been laid up under the protection of the harbor's fort while being prepared for another run at the Americans. The *Constitution*'s captain, Silas Talbot, had pursued the vessel, but realized he could not sail into the shallow harbor at "Port Plate," as he called it. So he commandeered a smaller ship, one that had just left the harbor and was due to return soon, loaded it with Marines and officers, and ordered them to sail into the harbor, spike the fort's cannons, then seize the French ship and sail it away. And they did. "They ran alongside [the *Sandwich*], and boarded her, sword in hand, without the loss of a man, killed or wounded," Talbot wrote. "Perhaps no enterprize [*sic*] of the same moment was ever better executed."

To defuse the situation, President Adams sent three senior envoys—Charles Cotesworth Pinckney, Elbridge Gerry and John Marshall—to Paris for discussions with the French government. This was the XYZ Affair—so called after the three unnamed French agents sent by French foreign minister Talleyrand to negotiate with the American delegation—if by "negotiate" is meant a demand for a $250,000 bribe, another demand for a forced "loan" of $10 million or so because of perceived American disrespect toward France, and an apology from Adams for his unkind remarks concerning the wishes of the French government to be bribed before agreeing to negotiate. Meanwhile, Adams' great rival, Jefferson, a man almost John Kerrylike in his irrational affection for France, betrayed his own country by secretly writing to the French government and telling them to ignore Adams' emissaries until he could gain the White House. The men were kept waiting for weeks as the French attacks continued, more ships were seized, more men killed or beaten, more sailors imprisoned while the French government prevaricated and delayed.

When the XYZ plot was revealed to an angry public, the de facto war between France and America was very nearly made official. (Charles Pinckney's defiant slogan, "Millions for defense, but not one cent for tribute!" came from this conflict with France.)

Adams persisted in his search for a diplomatic solution and hostilities had largely ceased by 1801. In 1803, the United States, now with Jefferson as president, was able to consummate the Louisiana Purchase—but only after France, despite losing fifty thousand soldiers in the effort, failed to suppress the successful uprising of slaves in Santo Domingo, thus depriving France of a rationale for a North American empire. The French threatened an invasion of New Orleans, and Jefferson was forced to mobilize the nation for the second time in six years for war against France. Jefferson's suggestion that he may have to make an alliance with Britain against the French also helped change French policy.

Even during the War of 1812, a war fought mostly to protect America's sense of honor, the United States studiously avoided an alliance with an untrustworthy France against Britain. The reason: the man who did more than any other to shape modern France. By the time Napoleon was done wrecking Europe the way Jacques Chirac has tried to wreck the UN, NATO and the EU, Jefferson, retired and enough at peace with John Adams to write friendly letters to him, had finally come to see the little emperor pretty much the way we see Chirac:

> The Attila of the age dethroned, the ruthless destroyer of 10. millions of the human race, whose thirst for blood appeared unquenchable, the great oppressor of the rights and liberties of the world, shut up within the circuit of a little island of the Mediterranean, and dwindled to the condition of an humble and degraded pensioner on the bounty of those he had most injured. How miserably, how meanly, has he closed his inflated career! What a sample of the Bathos will his history present! He should have perished on the swords of his enemies, under the walls of Paris. . . . In civil life a cold-blooded, calculating unprincipled Usurper, without a virtue, no statesman, knowing nothing of commerce, political economy, or civil government, and supplying ignorance by bold presumption.

During the American Civil War, France was heavily invested in the Southern cause because it saw the conflict as a way to keep a strong, unified America from becoming a rival to France, not only commercially but also philosophically: The French had always viewed the American experiment as a kind of political triviality, lacking the zeal of France's off-with-their-heads approach to revolutionary purity and untempered by the kind of political chaos that had followed in the wake of the French Revolution.

Despite Lincoln's protests, France invaded Mexico in early 1862 after the Mexicans ceased repaying loans that France had made to them as part of their support of Mexico before and during the Mexican War. But the debt-collection business was a pretext. France's real ambition was to thwart American claims of "manifest destiny" implicit in the Monroe Doctrine and to unite Central and South American countries in a grand, French-led "Latin league." Creating an outpost on America's southern border seemed like a good way to start. More than thirty thousand soldiers were required to establish Napoleon III's stooge, Archduke Maximilian of Austria, as "emperor" of Mexico. After the Civil War, when the United States helped Mexican leader Benito Juarez in his campaign to overthrow the French regime, Maximilian's wife, the Belgian princess Carlota, rushed back to France to ask Napoleon's help in saving her husband. France backed down in the face of American threats. So Maximilian was abandoned, captured and executed; and Carlota went insane, pottering around Belgium until the late 1920s. By the time the French empire in Mexico collapsed on May 15, 1867, some fifty thousand lives had been lost.

Nearly ten years later, the gift of the Statue of Liberty by "the people of France" to the United States on the occasion of the centennial of American independence stumbled because of almost complete indifference to the project by the people of France. When the statue finally arrived ten years too late, it was because Americans agreed to foot the bill. (To repay this debt to France, by the way, would require a mere $250,000, not counting interest, which we'll forgo since France still has to repay the billions of dollars they owe us from World War I debt. When America asked for repayment, the French called the U.S. "Uncle Shylock" and refused to pay.)

By the end of the nineteenth century, after a disastrous war with Prussia, France was anxious to solidify her position in Europe. The French saw the Spanish-American War in 1898 as an assault on European values—but especially on French financial interests. As a result, the lead-up to this war resembled the lead-up to the invasion of Iraq: The French, who held many Spanish IOUs, warned that attacking Spain would incur the wrath of "Europe" and probably result in an American defeat. As it happened, the war was conducted with few American casualties but with a great deal of publicity.

In World War I, after much debate, the American Expeditionary Forces, including my grandfather Claude and thousands of other American farm boys, arrived in France, wondering why the French army was mutinying, why Socialists were demonstrating for surrender in the streets of Paris, and why workers were striking at munitions plants. The French were unable to win a convincing victory until the Americans, under General John "Black Jack" Pershing, helped defeat the Germans in the Meuse-Argonne offensive, which led directly to the German surrender soon after.

My grandfather thought sending him to help France was one of Woodrow Wilson's many errors, and as a consequence he railed for the rest of his life against "the gol-darned Communist Republic of France." He could convincingly make "gol-darned" sound like an obscenity. I remember standing with him on the sidewalk in Red Cloud, Nebraska, home of Willa Cather, while my grandmother paid a visit to a doctor. An attractive girl passed by and he caught me looking at her. He rounded on me, his eyes narrowed, and in a loud, plaintive voice said, "Promise me, DB, that you'll never, ever go to that gol-darned Communist Republic of France."

The girl turned to look. In fact, people all the way down at the bank turned to look. I didn't promise, but I also didn't quite get the connection until one day, defying the wishes not only of my grandfather but also of the young woman who, at the time, was my first French girlfriend, I was quite literally run out of a small town in Brittany by her father, the village butcher. She had warned me that he sincerely hated Americans. That made no sense to me. How could you hate *all* Americans? I thought I could charm him, but I never got the chance. I said, "Bonjour!" and he chased me down the street in his bloody apron with a cleaver in his hand, just like in the movies.

The Second World War was a short one for most of France. In May 1940, after months of listening to the French boast of their impregnable Maginot Line, the Germans invaded by simply going around the stupid thing. The following month, France surrendered. For the most part, Vichy France endured the Nazis peacefully, doing more than their share to dutifully scour Europe of Jews, shipping them to death camps from a sports facility in Paris—and not stopping until a few days before the city was liberated by the allies.

The Vichy government was embraced as an enlightened regime, one in which rational neutrality, national virtue and prudent pacifism were combined. It was seen by most French citizens as morally and practically superior to regimes less cooperative with the Germans. Most of the French elite were content to serve Vichy and the Germans—and this included the left, as long as the Stalin-Hitler agreement remained intact: Some of France's most prominent Communist leaders worked for the Nazis. Only when Germany invaded Russia did the French left awake to the moral repugnancy of Hitler. The vast majority of France's future ruling class, from Hubert Beuve-Méry, the founder of *Le Monde,* to François Mitterrand, were Vichy collaborators. Jean-Paul Sartre, France's celebrated left-wing, anti-American nihilist, switched sides only when the Allies arrived in the suburbs of Paris. Whatever Resistance existed

11

was quickly dispersed—some say annihilated—by De Gaulle and by the Communists, who were both anxious to rewrite history and put their own men in place as the "official" Resistance. Despite the fiction of French hostility toward Germany, far more Frenchmen actively supported the Nazis than actively resisted them.

By the end of the war, France had been weakened by two world conflicts, chronic governmental instability and a depression. The nation's greatest threat, De Gaulle determined, came not from Nazis nor from Communists but from the Americans. America, after all, was the only winner in World War II: everybody else, with the possible exception of the USSR, had either lost or not won. But if the USA was the world's most powerful nation, De Gaulle felt it was also one whose military leaders had ridiculed him and whose political leaders had tolerated him only reluctantly. De Gaulle was a big man—nearly six and a half feet tall—and all of it was ego. France, De Gaulle decided, was entitled to nearly as much *gloire* as De Gaulle himself. Neither would ever surrender to a triumphant America. So on June 6, 1944, as Allied troops stormed the beaches of Normandy, De Gaulle—who had been excluded from the D-Day planning because the Allies distrusted him—launched a cold war fought with more tenacity than France had ever exhibited before.

De Gaulle could have been France's Churchill. Instead, he was its Tito. Even before Germany was defeated, De Gaulle was busy creating what in effect became a jagged second front in the Cold War, playing the Soviets against the British and the Americans, and playing the Arabs against Israel and the United States, more than once betraying his supposed allies in the process. French reliability as an American "ally" against Russia was so absurd that even popular films of the time, such as Hitchcock's *Topaz,* could build entirely plausible plots based on French perfidy and betrayal.

De Gaulle felt that in the great project of refashioning the story of French glory, the Americans must play no more than a minor role. Thus was born the myth of the Maquis, the French underground that became one of the great political fictions of the twentieth century. But what about all those American hospitals, soldiers and civilian officials working for NATO in postwar France? The expulsion of NATO in 1966 came as part of an anti-American policy that was not understood simply because to most Americans, it was so surprising, mystifying, irritating—even if ultimately insignificant.

In the entire history of French-American relations, there has never been friendship—only deceit, exploitation and animosity on the part of the French, and naïveté and indifference on the part of America.

2.

The French war with America is perhaps the only passive-aggressive grudge-match in human history. In the immediate aftermath of Normandy, it was fought with equal and sometimes allied fervor by both the Gaullists and the Communists, and it continues to this day as the animating principle behind French foreign policy. It defines France's role in the world and colors the way the French prefer their Americans—mostly as loudmouthed buffoons, caricatures, cartoonlike yahoos. It isn't accidental that faux-shucks multimillionaire docu-ranter Michael Moore is France's favorite American, usurping a position held for generations by Jerry Lewis. When Moore travels through Europe and tells the foreign press that Americans are "the dumbest people on the planet," the French government cheers and golden palms are strewn in his path. In France's war with America, Michael Moore is the new Jane Fonda, although his breasts are bigger. (One of France's favorite French comedians, meanwhile, is a guy who dresses up like an Orthodox Jew and struts around the stage imitating a Nazi in the service of Israel.)

Dehumanizing the enemy in war is a standard tactic. To implement this strategy, France has a Yankophobic press eager to help the national cause. Even a casual glance at the front page of *Le Monde* demonstrates the new moral math of modern France: Abu Ghraib=Auschwitz. Iraq=Vietnam. Bush=Hitler. The images from the Baghdad lockup at Abu Ghraib were a special treat for France. Of course, seeing a handful of bad American soldiers as symbols of American culture is how racists think whenever they see a black gang terrorize a subway train in the south Bronx. But in France, it's the way history is written, redacted, and written again.

Most of that revised history revolves around the uniquely nationalistic vision advanced deliberately by De Gaulle even before the wartime liberation of his sorry state was complete. De Gaulle's work was certainly in the French tradition: The revolution had caused France to become a nation without a distinction other than the reckless violence and hollow platitudes of their revolution.

The revolution did, however, differentiate France from other European nations, most of which were appalled by the barbarity of the French uprising and its subsequent surrender to its own Terror.

Shunned by the rest of Europe, France began the long process of giving tangibility to the arrogant concept of French exceptionalism, first by engaging in eccentric trivialities—creating a novel calendar, for example—then by implementing policies that first celebrated constant warfare and diminished God to the stature of a short Corsican; then centralized power in the state, diminished the role of the individual, and established a ruling elite; and finally, and consequently, conjured governments often out of thin air— the Terror giving way to a republic which became an empire then a monarchy, then a republic and on and on. It was an epoch in which the term "French victory" became an oxymoron. There was no postrevolutionary "golden age" of French politics. Instead, it was one damned thing after another—until you get here, to Paris, France, where the corrupt, felonious ex-mayor, Jacques Chirac, lounges in the Elysée Palace discussing the finer points of political logic—and worrying about his inevitable fall from power—

14

with his former prime minister and best political ally, Alain Juppé, who can no longer participate in French politics because he was found guilty of fraud, and his faithful cronies, including his son, all of whom have made millions through the banal expedient of mundane corruption involving everything from local public housing to global oil scams.

After more than a dozen substantial constitutional transformations, three monarchies, two empires, various experiments in terror and anarchy, five republics and a fascist puppet government, France now prides itself on its rational approach to government by decree and its economic model of national socialism. The evolutionary process of French civic development has left blood on the streets every time a new political creature has emerged from the slime of French history. Yet France presumes to offer the world a more civilized alternative to American leadership. It's a national myth, one the ruling elite knows must never be disbelieved and therefore one the French press has a critical role in maintaining.

■ ■ ■ ■ ■

IN FRANCE, THE PRESS IS THE REPOSITORY of conventional wisdom, such as it is. Unlike the free press in the United States or Britain, the French press enjoys heavy subsidies from the government (another handout of $400 million or so was announced late in 2004). In return, French dailies, regardless of political persuasion, report only the news that supports the fiction of French exceptionalism and superiority. Events that demonstrate otherwise are simply ignored. This convention of *silence* is well known but goes largely unnoted. As a result, the events of the world often contrive to reduce the French press to ridiculous insignificance.

Take, for the sake of illustration, the case of Alain Hertoghe, a French-educated Belgian and a seventeen-year veteran of *La Croix*, France's prestigious Catholic daily, where he worked as a senior editor. Every day during the opening phase of the war in

Iraq, *La Croix,* like all the papers in France, blossomed with the grim news of American and British defeats, the rising hatred of Americans by the Iraqis, the heroic struggle of Saddam—who, after all, was an old friend and business partner of France and a "personal friend" of Chirac himself. But then, suddenly, Baghdad falls. No armies are lost in the sand. The Ba'athist fascists dissolve into thin air. Could it be a miracle?

Well, France is a secular state, so no. But it's not a scoop, either, since most people—other than the French, the Germans and those who relied on the BBC—understood with clarity exactly what was happening in Iraq. In any case, journalist Hertoghe had been reading the Associated Press and Agence France-Press wires and comparing the news there with the twisted news he saw in his paper and others—and realized the story wasn't the victory of the Coalition in Iraq, but the defeat of the French elite and their carefully controlled media. The war that the national press had been fighting was lost in an ambush by reality.

Hertoghe saw that a serious wrong was being done by the French media. He said one particular news item pushed him over the line—an editorial cartoon in *Le Monde* claiming that President Bush's actions in Iraq had racist motivations. "It was very wrong," said Hertoghe. "To us in France, it reminded us of Le Pen." It had been preceded by many similar graphic slurs, including cartoons showing American troops stomping on dead babies and comments comparing the United States to terror states and to al-Qaeda. "I had already seen this [spinning of the news] happen in Afghanistan," he said. "It was the same then. I couldn't believe it was happening again the same way." Hertoghe thought there was a story in the media manipulation, so he wrote a book about it. And that's when his problems started.

Hertoghe was forty-four at the time and deputy editor of the online version of *La Croix.* His book, *La guerre à outrances: Comment la presse nous a désinformés sur l'Irak* (roughly, and more pointedly, "All-out war: How the press lied to us about Iraq"), was published by Calmann-Lévy, France's oldest publishing house, with impeccable timing in October 2002, just as several other introspective books critical of Paris-think were flourishing on the bestseller lists and stimulating debate among the yakking classes. But there was one little thing different about Hertoghe's book. It wasn't critical of France or of French politicians. It was critical of the French *press*.

Specifically, it was critical of the misleading and incompetent reporting that appeared not only in his own paper, but also in *Le Figaro, Le Monde, Libération* and the largest regional newspaper, *Ouest-France,* during the first few weeks of the war in Iraq. Hertoghe's book appeared in bookstores around the country and he waited for the debate to begin.

It never did. Instead, Hertoghe said, "I experienced collective and spontaneous silence." Other than a paragraph in a column in *Le Figaro* and an item in a free paper distributed to commuters, no major French newspaper reviewed the book or even mentioned it. The closest Hertoghe got to a media breakout was a radio interview, a television appearance and a piece in *Libération* by Daniel Schneidermann—a journalist fired by *Le Monde* a few months earlier for making critical remarks in a book of his own about the corruption of his paper's management and its apparent willingness to trade editorial favors for money.

The silent treatment surprised Hertoghe. "I was excited that I would be challenged on whether my book was fair," he said, "because I knew I had been fair. I hoped for a debate. But instead . . ." Instead, just before Christmas 2003, Hertoghe was confronted by his editor, Bruno Frappat, who told him that he had "committed an act of treason." Then he was lined up against the wall and fired.

So a veteran journalist, a chap who had covered the first Gulf War, who had crisscrossed America covering the 2000 election, and who wrote refreshing, somewhat iconoclastic pieces on a regular basis for a newspaper that prided itself on what Hertoghe called "the kind of tradition of freedom of thought that exists among Catholics" had been silenced for pointing out incompetence in his own profession.

Now normally, in French journalism, that sequence of events would have opened the door for the country's only interesting paper, the semi-satirical, left-wing *Canard Enchaîné*. As Stanley Hertzberg, a retired director of *Wall Street Journal Europe,* pointed out, the daily press, and especially *Le Monde,* has no tradition of good, independent journalism. *Canard* breaks most of the good political stories, which then come out in *Le Monde* or someplace else the next day, once it's safe to report them. "They [mainstream journalists] know that if they break the story, they might get in trouble."

But on Hertoghe, *Canard* wouldn't quack—even though *Canard*'s editor in chief, Claude Angeli, described Hertoghe's sacking as *"stupide à la part de* La Croix."

And *stupide* to stay silent on the part of other French dailies. Because Hertoghe's firing so clearly demonstrated not only the ideological, anti-American corruption of the French media, but also (and more importantly to journalists) the banal irrelevance of the mainstream media generally. Hertoghe's story has been told around the world, one paper at a time, like a platformed movie allowed to grow its own buzz. The *Wall Street Journal* ran a Boxing Day 2003 editorial called "Muzzled in Paris" that would have been a Suzy Menkes piece if it had run in the *International Herald Tribune.* But instead, the *IHT* followed, a few days later, with a John Vinocur piece that sparked an AP report that ran in papers everywhere. Political Euro-blogs, such as *Eursoc,* got hold of the story, so it was passed around in electronic samizdat. And a few days after that, the *Guardian* ran a piece on the affair, followed twenty-four hours later by a *Daily Telegraph* report. In his native Belgium, Hertoghe's story was big news, and even Bill O'Reilly tried to nab him for an interview, which Hertoghe declined. ("I thought it would just be to bash France," he explained.) In each of these reports and others, the message was clear: The elite French press had lied to their readers, and when somebody called them on it and blew the whistle, they buried him in silence and private ridicule, all of which, in the long run, simply added more tarnish to the cheap pot metal that constitutes journalism in France.

Still, Hertoghe was surprised at his fate. "I did not think *La Croix* would fire me. But I am not a pessimist. I am interested in seeing if this discussion [on French journalistic failures] will begin. And I am interested in knowing whether or not there is room for somebody like me in the French press." (There's not. Hertoghe now works for the French version of Yahoo! News.)

■ ■ ■ ■ ■

IN FRANCE AS ELSEWHERE, native journalists are taken most seriously only by other journalists. Happily for Hertoghe, his story gave everyone associated with French journalism a chance to expound on the frailties of the national press, a much-despised, notoriously vain, ludicrously self-protecting institution. Theories sprout like Kansas wheat about why newspapers have remained silent on a subject that so deeply reveals their own failures. Yet no one is terribly shocked. After all, the idea of one newspaper turning on another is unthinkable in France. Daniel Schneidermann's very occasional anti–*Le Monde* pieces in *Libération* are rare exceptions.

Some think the explanation is more practical. "The press in this country is in terrible financial shape," said Calmann-Lévy's editorial director, Ronald Blundel. "One well-aimed attack could result in one of [the national dailies] disappearing. They share a common vulnerability, so their response is to cover each other's back. If one large newspaper *really* went after another, there would be blood on the walls."

Hertoghe explained away the silence by looking at his own experiences. "Print journalists consider themselves to be an aristocracy," he explained. They look down upon their colleagues in radio and television—"the print journalists are paid less than the TV journalists and this makes them feel superior"—and on most of their countrymen. A print journalist turning against his own is a violation of the code of honor that binds thieves and French reporters.

And it's true: Ultimately, any attack on the media anywhere is seen as an assault on the organism in whose belly all journos dwell. The impulse to protect their own infects journalists everywhere, so liberal American journalists based in France jumped to the defense not of Hertoghe, but of their friends on the papers he was criticizing. One television correspondent pointed out that Hertoghe would have been fired by any American network if he had done something similar. (That may be true: just ask Bernard Goldberg, formerly of CBS, or Bob Zelnick, formerly of ABC.) Another American correspondent denied there was any conspiracy of self-protection in the French media. He was with French journalists in Iraq, he said, and he noticed they were "very fair in reporting civilian deaths." According to him, the reason there was silence surrounding Hertoghe's book is that the idea behind it is "shit."

"The problem is, French journalists are afraid," said Stanley Hertzberg. "Look at what happened to Hertoghe. That pretty much says it. Journalists here are afraid to do good journalism because they could lose their jobs, their credentials, their contacts. It's hard to get a good job in the French press."

The close relationship between the French press and the government certainly isn't new. In the 1970s, when writer and editor Harry Stein was a young co-editor of the *Paris Métro,* a weekly English-language paper in Paris, the editors commissioned a piece examining why the French press had played dead after an important political figure, Jean de Broglie, had been murdered. "It should have been the Watergate of France," Stein said. Instead, the story had been completely suppressed.

In pursuing the story, the *Métro*'s reporters discovered the reason why: It turned out that journalists routinely were helped by the government to find cheap apartments, fix traffic tickets, get free transportation, gain entrance for their kids into prestigious schools. That relationship hasn't changed in the last thirty years. Hertzberg was at the *Métro* in those days and remembers the climate well. "Sometimes we had reporters from the French newspapers bring us stories they were afraid to show their editors," he said. He was so incensed over the treatment of Hertoghe that he took his complaint to Reporters sans frontières, a group ostensibly dedicated to protecting journalistic freedom. He's still waiting for a reply.

The Hertoghe tale, said Hertzberg, "is shameful, in terms of freedom of the press. If this goes down, then everybody will have learned the lesson: Shut up."

Not to be cruel, but ultimately perhaps the explanation is cultural. "Look, France is a country of compromise," one media executive told me. "It's the basis of this culture. Saying one thing while doing another is a way of life here. Cynical behavior is seen as chic. To be called a cynic is to be given a compliment."

"The media took all their cues from Chirac and forgot the rules of their profession," Ronald Blunden agreed. Chirac wanted the United States to lose in Iraq, so "they reported this losing campaign, and even when, after six months, the facts proved them wrong, they did nothing to change their story. They made no effort to report the facts." Consequently, said Blunden, "France has the media it deserves [and] the French are absolutely unanimous in their opposition to the war in Iraq."

■ ■ ■ ■ ■

WHATEVER THE EXPLANATION for the silence surrounding Hertoghe's claims, to Blunden and others, the instinct of the French press for herd protection is rooted in reality. Newspapers are not a big business in France. Nobody reads the things: in a nation with a population of 60 million or so, the largest paper is the liberal *Le Monde,* with a circulation of less than 400,000. *Libération,* predictably left-wing, but broadly speaking a better and more interesting paper, circulates less than half that. Most readers of *Le Monde,* the centrist *Le Figaro* and *Libération* are political partisans looking for a daily dose of validation, and the kind of faux intellectuals who explain away French Muslim anti-Semitism by blaming it on Israel. If you're French and you want the news, you turn on the TV. In my little village, the largest-selling paper by far is the daily sports rag. By contrast, Germany's national dailies have huge circulations. In Britain, the daily circulation of the *Sun* alone is more than twice the combined daily circulation of every major national newspaper in France.

French newspapers are the captives of one of the strongest unions in France, the Communist-led CGT, which, like an old-fashioned Italian fascist union, simply strong-arms newspapers for cash—a deal going back to the days following the liberation—and terrifies them into silence, not that that takes much. "As a result," Blunden said, "the press in this country has never had the money, never had the finances to become truly independent, because eating away at the bottom line was the need to write the unions this huge check." In addition, France is one of the few nations in the world where newsstand distribution is controlled by a monopoly, the NMPP. In other words, if French papers made money, Rupert Murdoch would own a few.

3.

The French war on America is not about the seizure of land or wealth. It's about pride—the French sense of *gloire,* that bizarre Gallic combo of *gravitas* and elitist nationalism, a result of Napoleonic grandeur and Gaullist invention—and a desire to isolate America from Europe and diminish American influence: cultural, economic and military.

These are not objectives that require thousands of good marksmen. In fact, the easy part of waging war French-style is that you don't actually have to win the battles, because the confrontation with the enemy is never direct. The objective is less that you win than that your enemy loses. Although France has reopened its embassy and recognized the legitimacy of the post-Saddam government in Baghdad, for example, the French know there can be no victory in Iraq until there's an American defeat—which, in this context, means apologizing to France and paying off the losses incurred when trade with Saddam was disrupted. If France ultimately is successful at making the United States toe the multilateral line, France will have won in Iraq *and* in Europe.

In the months leading up to the invasion, Paris fought the war on behalf of Iraq against the Americans on two fronts—one in New York at the United Nations, where France effectively destroyed whatever small value the UN had left, and the other in the Middle East, where France sought to increase its influence by agitating against the United States and encouraging others to do the same.

Dominique de Villepin, the French foreign minister who looks and acts suspiciously like Bill Maher with a sense of humor, was a high-profile traveler in those days and weeks before the war. He believed very deeply in the Gaullist notion of *gloire,* and wore his belief like a piece of cheap jewelry. "He still seems torn between a career in government service and the romantic life of a poet," gushed an eager Robert Graham in the *Financial Times.* "*At his own expense,* he has published four volumes of poetry.... He has also written a book on Napoleon and just before his present job wrote a florid essay in a Gaullist vein on the need for France to rediscover its path of glory ... [emphasis added]." Among the titles on the Villepin shelf of classics: *Élégies barbares* (Savage Elegies)—that would be a poetry title—and *Le cri de la gargouille* (The Cry of the Gargoyle), which is the "florid essay."

His missions abroad weren't about applying pressure on Saddam Hussein to respond to Security Council resolutions. That would be absurd, since the French, along with the Russians and the Chinese, were on the Iraqi payroll, as recent reports have revealed. Villepin's missions were about lining up anti-American sentiment and flexing the EU muscle to keep that part of the Third World in awe of the French. When Morocco, for example, sought closer trade ties with the United States, France threatened to make their trade with the European Union much more difficult, so the Moroccans surrendered. The same extortion scam was used over and over as France engineered an ambush of the U.S. that would lead to a catastrophic American diplomatic defeat at the UN, one that would make it difficult to implement American foreign policy objectives there and elsewhere for years into the future. The French hope: an American surrender to the forces of French-led multilateralism.

The French strategy in this battle of their long-term war is outlined in fascinating detail by Kenneth Timmerman in his recent book, *The French Betrayal of America*. According to Timmerman, it involved having Chirac urge Bush repeatedly to come before the UN, promising French cooperation and support. He was finally successful in convincing Bush to seek UN approval. Villepin, meanwhile, was telling essentially the same story to Colin Powell, the U.S. secretary of state, in order to set him up for the public humiliation at the UN that took place on January 20, 2003, before a special session of the Security Council that had been convened at Villepin's insistence. He had successfully convinced the foreign ministers of Security Council members to attend, supposedly to discuss terrorism. But he used the meeting instead to lambaste U.S. plans for using force to make Iraq comply with all those UN Security Council resolutions. The entire UN debacle was the result of a French plan that had been put into play months before the final Security Council collapse, and into which the United States marched blindly.

Its purpose? First and foremost, to protect the heavy investment that France had in Iraq, France's Saudi Arabia, where Saddam was a huge buyer of French weapons and technology, and a kindly oil merchant to French oil companies, such as Elf. In the Oil-for-Food scandal that is still unfolding at the UN, the French play a significant role, having pocketed perhaps hundreds of millions by aiding Saddam's efforts to siphon off cash that today supplies arms to militant Islamic fascists waging war on the citizens of Iraq.

Bill Gertz, in his book *Treachery*, explains the military relationship between France and Iraq, one that is exactly parallel to the French relationship with Rwanda before, during and after the genocide there:

> An initial accounting by the Pentagon in the months after the fall of Baghdad revealed that Saddam covertly acquired between 650,000 and 1 million tons of conventional weapons from foreign sources. The main suppliers were Russia, China and France.
>
> By contrast, the U.S. arsenal is between 1.6 million and 1.8 million tons.
>
> As of last year, Iraq owed France an estimated $4 billion for arms and infrastructure projects, according to French government estimates. U.S. officials thought this massive debt was one reason France opposed a military operation to oust Saddam.
>
> The fact that illegal deals continued even as war loomed indicated France viewed Saddam's regime as a future source of income.

Gertz also reports on the French weapons used by Iraqis to kill Americans, to bring down Coalition aircraft and to defend the Ba'athist regime. If those French weapons aren't now in the hands of "rebel insurgents" who are killing Americans, kidnapping Italian women and beheading Turkish truck drivers, it isn't because France did a consumer recall. According to Gertz, French weapons were still being shipped to Iraq as late as January 2003—about the time Villepin arranged his little charade at America's expense.

But on another, equally important level, the reason for the French diplomatic and clandestine warfare against the United States was to solidify Chirac's popularity in France. As it had done for Germany's Gerhard Schroeder, the plan worked brilliantly. Chirac's popularity soared, while the UN's credibility—as bogus a concept as "Franco-American friendship" anyway—crashed and burned.

Chirac knew what Powell and other American leaders should have realized: anti-Americanism is now the Ecstasy of the European liberal bourgeoisie, the drug of choice for politicians feeling a little low in the polls. Like all drugs, it makes you stupid, but its feel-good appeal is undeniable. In Germany and France especially, politicians have astonished themselves at their ability to get really, really, totally high in the polls by simply hiding their fundamental incompetence behind a burning American flag.

It works. Even as the Coalition was fighting Saddam's henchmen on the outskirts of Baghdad, Frenchmen were vandalizing the graves of the Allied war dead on the coast of France, telling the Brits, via graffiti, to get their polluting "rubbish" out of French soil. Thanks to the French media and the nation's grandstanding politicians, one out of every three French citizens went to bed at night during the war dreaming of an American defeat in Iraq.

■ ■ ■ ■ ■

MORE BOOKS LIKE Timmerman's and Gertz's will no doubt appear soon on bookstore shelves, offering analysis of who did what to whom in Iraq. But an interesting view of what happened there—and what is still going on—can also be had by thumbing through stacks of French newspapers and looking back at this most recent outbreak of French warfare on the United States.

On April 5, American troops reached Baghdad. Within days, the city fell almost without a fight. Looting broke out spontaneously on the eastern edge of the city. The story of liberation was examined by the French press (as by the rest of the media) in terms of the confusion that followed the collapse of the Ba'athist regime. Immediately, in the French press and in the left-wing media elsewhere, the United States became a criminal state. A local UN representative, one Veronique Taveau, complained to *Libération* that "the inaction of the occupying forces" in the face of looting was a "violation of the Geneva Convention," while other newspapers wondered what the Americans were doing with all their newfound free time besides watching looters cart away office equipment, because everyone in the media business knows that chaos and catastrophe have a longer shelf life than crowd-waving and statue-tipping any day. For the French, in 2003 as in 1945, the scenes of American victory—in this case, jubilant Iraqis welcoming American Marines—had to be erased as quickly and as completely as possible.

Chirac and Villepin did not expect Saddam's Frenchified army to collapse with such efficiency. The rapidity of the war sent French diplomats scurrying through Araby to convince the leaders of the region to reward France's anti-American position with what an embarrassed *Berliner Zeitung* called "affection and orders." The media coverage in France continued to stress angry Iraqis and lunatic looters, and avoided those awkward men, women and children greeting their liberators. The anti-American side in France (and you could have invited the other side over to your studio apartment for dinner) was deeply disappointed that the war went so badly for them, and especially that the Iraqis had produced such an unseemly display of gratitude to the Coalition. The French knew that Americans now saw them as a deceitful "partner," one not soon to be forgiven. Consequently, many in Paris echoed the concerns expressed in *Libération* that the expansion of the European Union to admit so many pro-American governments into Europe might not be a great idea. One French deputy was quoted in the press saying that "Jacques Chirac must admit that the courage of the Americans and the English has brought a dictatorship to an end."

But the instant collapse of Saddam's regime had surprised Chirac and he feared that events might shove into the foreground those ugly domestic issues that could erode his amazing poll numbers. Even though 84 percent of French voters said he was right to oppose America, Chirac felt he was at risk because of what the *Guardian* called a "backlash from his peace campaigning." The paper reported that "after warnings from his own party that France had gone too far in opposing Britain and the U.S., [it] now faced international isolation."

■ ■ ■ ■ ■

FOR A WEEK OR SO after the fall of Baghdad, all of Europe was caught up in a big group blush. *Le Monde* pointed to Germany's embarrassment at backing a losing proposition and not only the demos by Kurds waving Stars-and-Stripes and Union Jacks and filling the streets of Nuremberg, but also the dejection of antiwar Germans in Berlin. *Le Figaro,* the newspaper most closely aligned to Chirac's right-center party, celebrated the fact that at least France wasn't Russia, where Vladimir Putin hastily convened a bizarre "antiwar" summit in St. Petersburg. France would be there, said a straight-faced *Le Figaro,* since it is France's destiny to bring peace to the relationship between France's "natural allies." The purpose of the meeting was to "reaffirm with one voice" the urgent need for the UN to take over for the Coalition in Iraq *right away* in order to safeguard the citizens—and, uh, to help take attention away from all those documents that were starting to surface showing that the Russians had been spying on Tony Blair and others for Saddam (and even doing some helpful recruiting of hit men that the Iraqis could hire).

Then there unfolded a great scene with the three of them on a small stage. Putin was carrying a big piece of lumber on his shoulder. He turned around and the board first conked Jacques in the noggin, then Gerhard! Bonk! Bonk! Just kidding, but as it happens, the leaders couldn't actually agree on their one-voice document, if only because they were speaking out of six sides of their collective mouths. No matter. The valiant effort was praised in a *Le Monde* editorial, and it received lots of play on French TV, where scenes of Baghdad looting continued to run, accompanied by lengthy passages read from the Geneva Convention, which to French politicians is like *The Hobbit*.

And eventually, the documents floated to the surface anyway. First, a *Daily Telegraph* reporter, David Blair, came across documents in a burned-out Iraqi ministry that seemed to implicate George Galloway, the left-wing MP from Glasgow, in a really ugly deal to exchange money (Saddam's) for influence (Galloway's). Galloway is a sort of British version of Michael Moore, but without a movie deal (for now). The files showed that Galloway apparently received hundreds of thousands of pounds of Oil-for-Food money channeled to him through intermediaries. Galloway had already been accused of milking the Miriam Fund, a charity seemingly intended to help sick Iraqi children. Then came more documents, this time found in the trashed offices of the Iraqi intelligence service, that showed a clear link between Saddam and al-Qaeda. The story so disturbed the vehemently antiwar BBC World Service that they dispatched the grotesque Judy Swallow, their very best anti-American sneer merchant, to suggest to her listeners that just *maybe* the press was making all this stuff up. But even Swallow's on-air expert, one of the BBC's peculiar "analysts," refused to go that far, leaving her to cast innuendos into the deep all by herself. As practitioners of unbiased journalism, many of the World Service's presenters suck, though none so much as Swallow.

The big payoff came when the *Sunday Times* published the result of its own scavenger hunt: the French had been routinely supplying the Iraqi government with intelligence on U.S. activities, including the contents of conversations between Chirac and Bush—thus joining the Germans and the Russians in being implicated in anti-U.S. espionage by documents found in the trash in

Baghdad. Other British newspapers published more evidence of French complicity with Saddam's regime. The news in France was different, of course. *Le Nouvel Observateur*'s headline: "English newspaper accuses the French of collaboration." The rest of the French press ignored the story and instead ran those photos of Chirac that make him look like the drunk VP at the office Christmas party.

■ ■ ■ ■ ■

IN FRANCE A KIND OF NERVOUSNESS SET IN as the nation's elite waited to see what would happen next. The press began murmuring about how bygones should be bygones. One paper took a look at the plight of U.S. soldiers in Iraq; the TV news began reflecting the reported "softening" of anti-Americanism among the French. *Le Figaro* even said it was time for France to come to the aid of her "oldest ally," and to send in French troops to help the Americans. Help them do what, exactly, wasn't explained, but surrender could certainly be inferred. Then some of the most terrifying photographs of Paul Wolfowitz ever published began appearing next to stories that said the United States was going to make France "pay" for its perfidy. An op-ed in *Le Figaro* by Richard Perle was headlined, "The Fall of the UN."

Libération meanwhile offered readers a trio of pieces reporting the effects of the American boycott of all things made in France. In a main story, the paper reported that poll numbers showed Americans were starting to feel about the French pretty much the way that the French had always felt about Americans—and, more importantly, how that translated to a serious decline in, among other things, wine exports to the United States, said to be worth some $1 billion a year. There was also an amusing Q&A with American economist and boycott backer Irwin Stelzer of the Hudson Institute. *Libération* clearly thought Dr. Stelzer was a lunatic: "You have written that 'English cheeses are good substitutes for

French cheeses.' Are you serious?" The third piece looked at the limits of the boycott, noting a deal made by Rupert Murdoch with Thomson, a French company—despite the fact that Murdoch's FOX News employs "motormouths" (*animateurs vedettes*) like Bill O'Reilly, who has said many clever but nasty things about the denizens of Fromageville. The *Onion*'s version of the American solution to the problem of a weasel-laden Security Council had China, Russia and France replaced by Condi, Rummy and Cheney. But that's exactly what happened, *oui?*

As the fall of Saddam looked more and more irreversible, Germany, France, Belgium and mighty Luxembourg immediately defaulted to plan B—a summit at which the formation of a European military force would be unveiled to act as a "counter" to America. It was ignored.

But then—a miracle! On April 18, 2003, a Friday, just when it appeared that the Americans and their allies had won the war in Iraq, ten thousand Muslims—all "resolutely hostile" to the United States, as *Libération* helpfully pointed out—appeared on the streets carrying banners telling the Americans to go home. For the French it was a happy reminder that from the moment Chirac had told the UN "no way," the war in Iraq had nothing to do with whether Saddam lost. That couldn't be prevented. It was about whether or not America could win. That war, the French happily noted, was just getting started.

If you're a cleric jockeying for power in post-Saddam Baghdad, *every* Friday's payday. So it wasn't surprising to see the faithful crowds pour out of mosques and into the streets following prayers that Allah would please send crowds into the streets to make sure that powerful government jobs went to guys who run mosques. Allah also carefully directed them past the representatives of the Infidel Media and gave them banners on which the creative spirit of Jesse Jackson had been mysteriously written: "No Bush! No Saddam! Yes! Yes! To Islam!" Sloppy scansion, maybe— but music to the ears of the president of France.

31

For months, since long before a shot had been fired in Iraq (not counting those noisy firing-squad volleys), there had been accounts of rising Arab anger toward the United States, stories about mullahs calling for jihad, and of French, German and Russian efforts to save Saddam's regime from the evil Americans. Then came the Coalition invasion and reports of angry Iraqis glaring at passing tanks, of looters gone wild, of Information Ministry-aided interviews, of unprovoked American atrocities, including a steady diet of interviews with anybody who claimed to have lost a loved one to a misdirected bullet, no matter who may have fired it. Like the Iraqi clerics, the French had been waiting patiently for their ship to come in. Their apparent hope was that if only enough street-churn could be created in Baghdad and other Iraqi cities either in advance of the Coalition victory or alongside it, the long defeat of America could finally begin.

For Chirac and Villepin, it became apparent that there were only four ways for France to gain a real win in Iraq.

- First, France would need to regain its role as principle beneficiary of Iraqi misfortune. A lot of money still hangs on this one.
- Second, the French felt that the infrastructure they had built in Iraq must be rebuilt by France and by no one else. But that would be difficult because, as the French press had already adroitly reported, the Americans had given the rebuilding job to Bechtel, among other American companies, and everybody knows that Bechtel is not French because financial audits have shown that it actually makes a profit. So even as the lights in Iraq went back on, the curtain came down on this scenario. Score one for America.
- Third, the weapons of mass destruction would have to be found by UN inspectors. To the entire planet, the WMDs were the beef. But even if they are someday found, unless they're Blix-discovered and Blix-certified, they cannot possibly be genuine. Odds are now five trillion to one against the Americans on this one.

- Fourth, Iraq would have to be turned into an anti-American mosh pit in order for France to triumph. The key to success here was getting radical Shi'ites into positions of power. The French have done what they can to further this one, including blocking any meaningful NATO involvement in training security personnel.

But even as Iraq slowly started to become the kind of U.S. headache that the Europeans had hoped for, they also had to deal with the hangover produced by their own anti-American excesses. Finally, Chirac figured maybe it was time to call Bush. So he picked up the phone—and rang Villepin instead because he knew Bush would never take the call. Villepin asked Jean-David Levitte, the perpetually offended French ambassador to Washington, to plead with Karl Rove to have George answer the phone when Jacques called. Meanwhile, Villepin got on the phone to Colin Powell and made the same plea. Finally, the call was put through. It lasted twenty minutes and was touted in France as friendly, but described in America as "professional." Wolfowitz told curious U.S. senators, "I think France is going to pay some consequences, not just with us but with other countries."

France launched a serious effort to convince itself that, really, Chirac's crazy ambush of American policy was just a friendly argument between friends. For proof, the French, who love philosophers, turned to a great intellectualizer, Jack Valenti, who in a *Figaro* Q&A headline shouted, "The Americans and the French must continue to get along!" Like frogs and legs, Jack.

■ ■ ■ ■

As THE COALITION TIGHTENED its control on Baghdad, France moved to secure its alliances in the region, especially its friendship with Syria. After Secretary of Defense Donald Rumsfeld asked the Syrians to please refrain from making chemical weapons and stop offering tourist visas to wayward Iraqi generals, the French press happily succumbed to the epidemic of chronic systemic apoplexy that swept through Paris.

The French saw the pain and suffering that the Bush administration caused the Ba'athist regime in Damascus as inexcusable. *Le Monde*, in an outraged editorial, asked why the Americans act so *American*. After all, both Syria and Iraq are Ba'athist fascists, so, according to the paper, it's only "logical that Iraqi Ba'athists took refuge" next door with Syrian Ba'athists. America couldn't possibly understand the joys of simple friendship like that. Besides, said the paper, it's not as if Syria had done anything wrong: "Having refused to sign anything, Syria, unlike Iraq ... is free to develop weapons of mass destruction. ... So why now the threats?" Exactly.

Le Monde had two explanations for the American bullying. Either it was part of a regional plan to "destabilize the most radical regimes" by putting them on notice that producing weapons of mass destruction and harboring terrorists are no longer acceptable policies. Or—and I think this just might have been the explanation that *Le Monde* was favoring—"the White House is drunk on military strength." *Le Monde* accused the United States of putting its own interests ahead of the interests of others, a concept unknown to France, of course.

Most of us knew that a war in Syria wasn't *really* the plan. We knew that if you have a big, victorious army sitting around, you might as well use it as a way of leveraging a little serious attention, no? *Non!* The reaction of the French, the Germans and the left-wing Brits shows why Europeans can't play poker, and instead prefer games of chance, like roulette and driving in Italy. The quintessentially American skill of turning a card and making a bluff is just lost on them.

But the French maneuver hit a snag, too. France had about as much credibility as the UN. This meant that anybody could play a busted flush and make a French poker player fold. For France, even sending Villepin to Syria was "playing a risky game."

Le Monde complained that the Americans mysteriously didn't seem to care anymore what Villepin did or said, while the Syrians apparently didn't take him very seriously, either. As the paper pointed out, the Syrians had to ask themselves, "If Washington leans on [us], what will France be able to do to help? Why would France be more effective in a Syrian crisis than in the Iraqi crisis?" Good questions.

Villepin's Damascus visit was just part of a blitz of Arab capitals to help clear things up, ease tensions and make the world once again safe for France. The French media reported that he did not publicly utter "America," "the United States of America" or "George Bush" for seventy-two straight hours, a new personal record. He listened politely, however, while others did: the Syrian foreign minister, for example, compared the "American occupiers" of Iraq to Nazi storm troopers while Villepin sat by impassively.

4.

How would events in Iraq have unfolded if we had done it French-style? It's hard to say, but there are some examples around.

For example, before the U.S. presidential election of 2004, candidate John Kerry announced that he had a "secret plan" for dealing with Iraq. Everybody wanted to know what it was. It turned out to be just like the "secret plans" I had back in high school when I'd take girls to the drive-in: No matter how much agonizing the scheme involved, nothing was going to happen.

Kerry's secret plan, it finally emerged, was to convince France and the UN to help us get out of Iraq. At a presidential debate, he told George Bush—a man who defends affirmative action better than he does a coherent foreign policy—that he would call for a summit and ask for help.

To you and me, asking France to help you win a war is like asking your poodle to break up a dogfight. But apparently Kerry felt that asking France to help win a war would make the war "sensitive" because, as everyone knows, France is more sensitive than the United States. (And never mind that both the French and the German governments have said repeatedly that no matter who is president of the United States, their troops will not set foot in Iraq. *"Ni aujourd'hui, ni demain"* is how the new French foreign minister, Michel Barnier, put it when asked if French troops would come to the aid of a Kerry-built alliance in Iraq.)

■ ■ ■ ■ ■

MAYBE IT'S JUST AS WELL. For a good model of how a sensitive, Frenchified foreign policy works, let's look at the warring, unhappy natives in faraway Darfur, a dusty stretch of the Sudanese way-outback. According to the U.S. Congress, there's been a genocide going on in Darfur for quite a while, and chances are it will still be going on when you read this page. But the good news: if we apply John Kerry's secret plan, it was all being handled just right.

In Darfur, Arab killers, backed by the Sudanese government, were cleansing the province of blacks by attacking villages, where they'd loot, rape, abduct, then ride off. Meanwhile, the blacks, who survived on desert shrubs, ran for their lives. This had all gone on for a very long time. One of the few respites from slavery, rape and cruelty that the Darfurians (or whatever they call themselves) have enjoyed was in 1877, when a great Christian hero, Charles George "Chinese" Gordon, the governor-general of Sudan at the time, arrived to suppress a conflict very much like the one raging there now. Except Gordon arrived alone on a camel, smoking a cheroot and demanding a prompt surrender. He got it.

Gordon was not French the way 7-Up is not cola. He was, however, later killed at Khartoum by Islamic fundamentalists when the British government failed to find the nerve to save him. (He thus became a historical figure of such magnitude that it took Charlton Heston to play him.) Darfur instantly returned to its hellish ways.

About two years ago, this long-running conflict appeared likely to morph eventually into an Ethiopian-scale disaster, something that would require the intervention of, say, *rock stars* if disaster was to be averted. For months, NGOs and various UN agencies, along with the Bush administration, kept warning that things were going to go very south in Darfur.

When the number of displaced reached a million or so, and when the dead numbered in the tens of thousands, and when the victims of rape and mutilation could no longer be counted at all, and when the entire population stood at the brink of starvation, and when all the rock stars couldn't go because they were busy planning to go out pimping for John Kerry, the United States did what Kerry said we should always do in order to wage a more sensitive campaign for democracy and justice. America went to the United Nations. Many empty gestures followed. The U.S. secretary of state stood in the middle of a big Sudanese nowhere, spoke softly and threatened the killers with the big Nerf stick: knock it off, he said, or face the wrath of the UN.

For weeks, while more and more people were being killed in Darfur, the Security Council debated just what should be done to convince the government of Sudan to stop supporting the Janjaweed militia, the band of Muslim brothers responsible for the slaughter. The United States wanted to move decisively, but the resolution offered by the Bush administration went off the tracks because it contained the word "sanctions." "Sanctions" is not a sensitive word. The reporting in the French-leaning press—which would include the *New York Times* and the *Boston Globe,* as well as the *Times'* expat paper, the *International Herald Tribune*—was thorough enough. Reporters such as the *Times'* Warren Hoge covered the debate carefully, except for one stray fact that somehow escaped attention: Exactly who on the Security Council had objected to the word "sanctions"? Who had thrown the process into the slow lane? And why?

I'll spoil the suspense here, because you already know the answer. It was the French. This news was not reported in the French press, either. To discover this fact on the same day that Hoge's piece ran, you had to catch a tiny comment in the *Frankfurter Allgemeine,* explaining that France, along with her allies, Russia and China, was guilty not just of trading blood for oil, as the French are always saying about the United States, but of trading "oil for corpses." Sudan, it turns out, sits on what some experts think is a huge pool of oil. And the French have an oil deal with Sudan, just as they did with Saddam Hussein. It took nearly a month of debate for the Security Council to issue a toothless warning: the sanctions threat would be removed and replaced with a threat to maybe impose them later. The government of Sudan dismissed the resolution as illogical and impractical. Few journalists noticed all this. Mark Steyn, however, writing in the *Daily Telegraph,* noted that Sudan was "getting away with murder."

And as of this writing, months later, they're still getting away with it. In fact, to make sure that sanctions couldn't happen quickly, the European Union looked into the entire conflict, then announced it had thought things over and yes, things were not nice in Darfur, but despite what the U.S. Congress and President Bush had said, what was happening in Darfur wasn't an actual *genocide*. It was, they said, just some severe unpleasantness. The EU would know. A genocide is the kind of thing the French helped engineer and arm and cover up in Rwanda in 1994—where under French surveillance and tacit support, some eight hundred thousand people died while France not only did nothing, but actively abetted the murderers, all merely to show support to a Francophone regime. If Darfur were a certified genocide, then international agreements would require the EU to actually *do* something. That is not the EU's sensitive way. And, as long as the French and the UN have a say, nothing is likely to change there in the immediate future— unless it's to make matters worse: In the spring of 2004, hepatitis broke out in the refugee camps.

Darfur is the kind of foreign policy the United States would have if it had followed the "secret plan" of John Kerry and catered to the French and German politicians who craved George W. Bush's defeat. If the French and the UN had had their way in Iraq, Saddam Hussein would still be tossing his people to his hungry wolfboys and looking for a way to get back at the United States. And who knows? Perhaps by now he would have been successful.

The French-centric press in New York and Boston, like the actual French press in downtown France, obviously preferred the UN's Darfur solution over Bush and Blair's Iraq solution—just as the French and the Germans preferred Kerry to Bush. The French certainly wanted no more Chinese Gordons—or even Colin Powells, for that matter—running around Sudanese oil fields making trouble. They know what they do want, and what they want is what they know.

■ In Darfur, the French want everybody to chill. Thus, Michel Barnier, the French foreign minister, played the humanitarian poseur in the pages of *Le Figaro*. His four action items: 1) look for an African way to fix it [*sic*]; 2) encourage dialogue; 3) encourage more dialogue; 4) congratulate France for its forward-looking policies.

■ In Iraq, they want quagmire. Thus, correspondents hang out, turn up their Jimi Hendrix CD, and send back context-free human-interest anecdotes straight out of Da Nang, '68—just like in the movies. (The big scoop of Anne Barnard, of the *Boston Globe,* was that a corporal in Iraq was pretty unhappy with being stuck in Iraq, by inference obviously the symptom of a much larger problem.)

Here's a secret plan: Every time you think it can't get worse in Iraq, take a look at Darfur. Or Bunia. Or Ivory Coast. Or anyplace else the UN is playing a peacekeeping role with French support.

■ ■ ■ ■ ■

AFRICA IS ACTUALLY A GOOD PLACE to examine France's other qualities as a partner in the big global conflicts. It might help you understand how a nation who is always first to insist on a share of power in determining the outcome of events in other, usually less fortunate, countries has behaved when left to its own devices.

Africa is the scene of some of France's greatest military victories in the last 190 years, since Napoleon's defeat at Waterloo. During the great scramble for African real estate, France was brilliant at pummeling native tribes and Saharan chieftains. Its famed Foreign Legion—fierce because they were *foreign*—helped secure an empire that stretched across some of the worst real estate in the Southern Hemisphere and was literally built on sand. When France's African expansion was checked by the British on the upper Nile at Fashoda in 1898—thus foiling France's efforts to cut the Cape-to-Cairo axis of British African colonialism—the event became a national trauma and gave permanence to France's little-guy diplomatic belligerence around the world.

Unburdened by the Anglo-Saxon requirement that government observe the rule of law, France's empire in Africa (and its rather more haphazard outposts in Southeast Asia and elsewhere) thrived on under-the-table deals and personal relationships that guaranteed a legacy of croissants, corruption and cynicism. France's ideal was to make its colonies essentially French. And they largely succeeded: Wherever the French have ruled, you can get good coffee, bribe an official and depend on anti-Americanism as a tenet of foreign policy.

In Africa, France really exceeded itself. Postwar independence mattered little to those living in former French colonies. The old ties remained, secured by clandestine scams and the ongoing military presence of French troops, ready to help whatever pal of Paris needed assistance. Jonathan Fenby, whose *On the Brink* is essential reading for anyone interested in modern France, nails it when he writes that after independence,

Big companies and political parties used friendly former colonial states as handy screens for below-board activities: smaller entrepreneurs set up all manner of businesses—from garbage collection to personal security. . . . For decades, France backed its favored dictators with 8,000 troops stationed across the continent and an equal number on standby at home. In all, [the French] have intervened on more than two dozen occasions since the 1960s to put down rebellions and mutinies, to prop up France's friends, and to perpetuate what the *Wall Street Journal* dubbed a "virtual empire." . . . At the height of the Rwandan tragedy, France helped to supply weapons to the massacring Hutus, who came to be known by the French terms of *les génocidaires,* and sent in troops to provide safe haven for the killers. . . . Some years later, *Le Figaro* quoted Mitterrand as having said that, in countries like Rwanda, genocide wasn't such a big thing.

Fenby also brilliantly writes a scene straight out of *Casablanca* when he reports Mitterrand's response to being informed of the degradations common in Francophone Africa: "I am surprised and pained to hear what I hear." Fenby concludes: "As if Mitterrand had no idea of the nature of his host when his helicopter deposited him on the deck of a dictator's yacht with its forty-place dinner setting in rose crystal . . . ."

France's financial scandals always have their African component, with French oil companies usually playing a leading role. In fact, if you're a Halliburton-conspiracy nut, you'll love Elf-Aquitaine, France's huge petroleum-based conglomerate. As the unfolding scandal reveals, some of France's richest and most powerful men have made their millions at the expense of Africa—Jacques Chirac foremost among them. The idea behind Elf, established by De Gaulle in 1963, was "to ensure France's independence in oil," but as *Le Monde* reported, the company quickly "lived, grew and prospered in a special and incestuous relationship with Africa," where it served as cash cow, spy agency, propagandist and bribe facilitator.

Because it is an affair of the elite, both the Socialists and the center-right are among the more than three dozen politicians and corporations thus far implicated in what is certainly France's biggest corruption scandal in two hundred years—or roughly since Napoleon questioned Josephine's fidelity. Already, some of Mitterrand's and Chirac's most trusted aides, ministers and supporters have been caught in the investigations. Mitterrand is dead, of course, but if there is any semblance of legal justice in France, when Chirac's term in office ends, his term in prison will begin. He's been saved from the slammer only by a law he had passed to give himself immunity from prosecution so long as he can cling to power. That could be quite a while. Chirac's strategy is to die in office, surrounded by all the chintz and poodles that the Elysée Palace can provide.

The corruption that flows from Africa into France flows back again. The consequences can be seen in recent French interventions there.

Rwanda. The tenth anniversary of the Rwandan genocide, in which 800,000 people were killed by their own government in a relatively short span of time, has come and gone. To commemorate the hideous event, the French are still conducting elaborate investigations trying to figure out how such a thing could happen. Here's my hunch: It happened because African politics are generally tribal and because the UN force was mired in corruption and incompetence, as the UN's own commander in Rwanda, General Roméo Dallaire, told a recent Paris press conference, and as Kofi Annan subsequently admitted to *Le Monde*. Dallaire, a Canadian, noted that there would have been more of an outcry if people had shot 800,000 mountain gorillas, instead of 800,000 humans. But the biggest reason such a thing happened is because the French not only allowed it, but colluded in the event itself. As Jonathan Fenby notes in *On the Brink*, as the genocide unfolded, the French continued to arm the killers while the U.S. and Belgium called for UN withdrawal. Other reports have shown that the French trained the killing squads themselves. Their reasons for doing this aren't particularly inspiring. The French were motivated most of all by the fear that usurpers might toss their Francophile regime out. It's not often that politically correct views are actually true, but the politically correct view of Africa says you can tell a good guy from a bad guy because the bad guy is the white guy. It may not always be true elsewhere, but it was certainly true in Rwanda, where the white guys spoke French, sold guns and helped cover up the atrocity as long as possible.

To make amends, the French are pressuring the European Union to fund the establishment of a big African army to the tune of $300 million. They can use the money to buy guns from France. That's how you say "twofer" in French.

Ivory Coast. The Ivory Coast conflict provides another example of how well the UN does under French supervision. In that once prosperous and calm corner of the Big Nowhere, happy Ivoirians once drove Mercedes and bought mutual funds, just like the rest of us. But then the tribes in the northern half of the country, who just happen to be Muslim, decided to wage war on the non-Muslims in the south.

Because Ivory Coast is in what France perceives to be its sphere of influence (they speak French in Abidjan, the Ivoirian downtown), France went to the UN and got its approval for something called "Operation Licorne" and, under Dominique de Villepin, brought the combatants together in something called the Marcoussis Accords. Then they started spending a million euros a day to give the whole show some special effects and the ring of truth.

After a year, the Agence France-Press surveyed UN sources and came up with a snapshot of what happens when you use the multilateral option that some liberals want for Iraq—i.e., France at the head of a UN peacekeeping force:

- *Social services and local government collapse.* " 'Basic social services, schools, health services, agriculture, trade, everything's getting worse,' said Besida Tonwe of the Office for the Coordi-nation of Humanitarian Affairs (OCHA)."

- *Disease rises.* "Illnesses that had been held in check are begin-ning to kill again and malnutrition, which was previously unthinkable in Ivory Coast, has reappeared."
- *Doctors vanish and hospitals close.* "In the north and west about 80 percent of health services are said to be not functioning and four-fifths of staff had not returned to their posts one year after the crisis broke."
- *Epidemic diseases re-emerge.* "Measles, meningitis and cholera have reappeared."
- *600,000 people are displaced.*
- *Refugees increase.* 300,000 immigrant laborers flee the country. So do at least 50,000 Ivoirians.
- *Schools fall into ruin.* Schools are closed, looted or overcrowded.
- *A bumper crop of orphans.* The number of AIDS orphans is expected to rise from 420,000 to 720,000 next year.
- *A famine in agriculture.* "Agriculture and trade have likewise been hard hit with a slump in income, causing general impov-erishment with all the predictable effects on nourishment and health of the population, say UN relief agencies, predicting a drop in next year's harvest."

France was a seriously conflicted leader in Ivory Coast. For one thing, France's Muslims are *all* on the side of the rebels—as Chirac's government discovered when it tried to arrest some of the rebel leaders in Paris, only to release them when Muslims in both Paris and the northern districts of the Ivory Coast conducted huge street squawks. For another, the typical French method of "peace-keeping" is to put soldiers on the ground, concentrate them in a small area, then declare peace in the place where the soldiers are—but not where they aren't.

The French fiction was that they were working with the rebels and the government to move the country back to a minimum of security, but in fact the government in Ivory Coast was entirely make-believe. Paul Bremer's Iraqi Governing Council was the Court of the Sun King in comparison. When one French journalist asked rhetorically, "If the French army leaves the Ivory Coast, how many minutes will the government survive?" the question sent Villepin into a fit of turbocharged platitudes.

Events in Ivory Coast have had a kind of surreal quality of late. One of the rebel factions with whom France was supposed to be working had a falling-out with the others. As a result, twenty-three people were killed in a provincial center when one group of rebels stormed a bank and others tried to move in on them. That incident caused France to even consider peacekeeping in places where there was no actual peace, instead of barricading themselves into safe compounds.

Twenty-three people in one afternoon in a country that had supposedly been under the care of French-led UN peacekeepers for a *year*. If it had been a GI tripping over a landmine in Baghdad, it would be a "spiral of violence and terrorism." But where all you had was a Reuters guy and an Agence France-Presse guy bumping into each other in a dash for cover, it was just another day in what Villepin called "the spirit of the Marcoussis Accords." Next, a French broadcast journalist was shot by a government supporter. Hysteria swept Paris.

Leaping with fairylike agility into the fray, Villepin wrote a gaseous plea for peace. To make sure the flamboyant document had the greatest possible impact on those who most needed Villepin's comfort, the poetic homily appeared in the pages of *Libération*. The bad news for the citizens of Abidjan? "For its part, France will continue to assume all its responsibilities." Or maybe that was the good news. Either way, in Ivory Coast, the French-brokered peace agreement between the Muslim rebels in the north and the government in the non-Muslim (for now) south crumbled bit by bit until finally France went back to the UN to ask for more help.

The four thousand French troops in Ivory Coast were joined by a small contingent of non-French "peacekeepers" who were mostly dispatched to the rough border separating the warring sides. The present situation is what you might call a "quagmire"— but only if you were a French journalist and only if you were reporting from Iraq.

Congo. Once, when I was younger and dumber, I flew as a load-master on a cargo plane over the civil war in Angola. The idea was to deliver some provisions from the Marxist government then in power in Luanda to the Cuban army that was helping the Angolan government hold onto a provincial town completely surrounded by rebel UNITA forces.

To get there, you flew above the clouds at thirty thousand feet or so until you got *directly* over the airport, then you did a dizzying descent in a very tight corkscrew approach. If you flew too wide, UNITA would shoot you. When we landed and started tossing off the groceries, I mentioned to somebody that the place must be kind of tense. "Oh no," he said. "Here, everything is peaceful." Then he pointed at some trees. "But over there, it's terrible."

That's the way the French brought peace to Bunia, a town in a particularly war-ravaged corner of Congo. More than fifty thousand had died and half a million were homeless there by the time the French arrived. They nailed down the city limits and kept the townsfolk from shooting each other, mostly, then declared everything to be peaceful. Meanwhile, down the road out of town, slaughter proceeded apace.

Next, the French handed over Bunia to an EU operation called "Artemis," still under French military command and as part of a UN mandate. French Defense Ministry spokesman Jean-François Bureau explained that the French "worked pragmatically and concretely to identify the resources and means needed, we considered there was no need to call for additional NATO assets. . . . It's an EU mission in the context of European security and defense policy, in conditions that it has consistently identified, that is, a case for which European forces have been gradually structured, a security mission for the UN." It was also the EU's first solo military deployment outside Europe.

Some four thousand troops were brought in—and the situation in Bunia deteriorated even more. In 2004, soon after the EU took over, a UN refugee camp housing some fifteen thousand people was attacked by Congolese militia. Women and children were hacked to death while the EU's peacekeepers, camped a few yards away, watched. Once the dying stopped, the peacekeepers went back to work, paying the young teenage girls who survived the massacre for sex. A UN-EU spokeswoman in Bunia told the BBC, "I have heard rumours on this issue. It is pretty clear to me that sexual violence is taking place in the camp. I have requested evidence and proof on this matter, but I have not received anything from anyone."

A few meters away, the BBC interviewed a thirteen-year-old mother who explained that the militia came into the camp and raped girls, like her, almost every night. A better bet, said a fifteen-year-old, was to go with the European troops: "The UN soldiers help girls like me, they give us food and things if we go with them."

The EU gave it up to the UN. Now, with MONUC, one of the UN's most expensive peacekeeping missions, there are more than ten thousand multinational soldiers on duty around the clock, sleeping with adolescent girls while uniformed UN MPs keep order in the makeshift brothels. Bunia is no Baghdad. Bunia is pure hell. And a Frenchman still runs the show.

5.

The Frenchman running the show in the 2004 U.S. presidential campaign, John Kerry, explained that the United States and the world would be safer if we enjoyed the military support of our "traditional European allies"—which to him did not mean Poland or Britain or Italy. It meant France and Germany.

It's interesting how the perception of foreign approval rein-forces America's domestic political views. For example, there's often something comforting about British approval if you're a hawk, and a similar coziness about French approval if you're a dove. In fact, the attitude you have toward France is probably determined by your political inclinations more than any piece of specific information. If you're a political conservative, France is anathema because of its duplicity and instinct for betrayal and its rejection of American claims of leadership. If you're a political lib-eral, chances are you think France is a little cranky, but charm-ing, and besides you like the whole communitarian, anticapitalist *gestalt* of the place, with its wine-and-cheese ambiance. It's like Wisconsin without those violent Packers. Those in the American media, by and large, are liberal, and therefore well disposed toward the French and their policies. Besides, the French say really nasty things about Americans—especially about American working-class people, people with religious convictions, Republicans, SUV drivers, beer drinkers and members of the NRA—so that's com-forting to many liberal American journalists.

A recent book, *Dangerous De-Liaisons,* makes all this embar-rassingly obvious. Ostensibly a "dialogue" between Jean-Marie Colombani, the pathologically anti-American editor of *Le Monde,* and Walter Wells, the New York Times Company's man in charge of editing the *International Herald Tribune,* the book is essentially the transcript of two charming men who have come together to agree to agree. Much binds them. Colombani is an important French insider, obviously. Wells is a well-known and well-liked expat American; an affable liberal, he has lived in France for a quarter-century. He and his talented wife are fixtures on the French social scene, rather like a well-behaved version of the Fitzgeralds. As a journalist, Walter is considered brilliant for having married Patricia, who is a fabulous gastronome, one of the most knowl-edgeable food writers on the planet, with her own business Web site at patriciawells.com. (There is no walterwells.com.) Walter

Wells has his job because the New York Times Company threatened to bankrupt the *International Herald Tribune* if the Washington Post Company didn't sell its 50 percent stake in the outfit. In an effort to make itself into a reputable global brand, the *Times* has pumped millions into the *Herald Tribune*—and right back out again. The paper loses millions every year.

Both men know each other and other members of the French elite very well. Both men think that France is marvelous and that George W. Bush is a right-wing nut. And both men think France has been wronged by hateful American zealots. To Wells, in fact, harsh criticism of France "is the response of simpletons" and the American reaction to French behavior concerning Iraq was just an excuse for the great unwashed to party:

> ... with Iraq as the catalyst, America slipped into a mode of France-bashing more virulent than ever. And it was not limited to the Joe Six-pack America, or to Fox News and the Murdoch press. It became pervasive—*Vanity Fair,* certainly no right-wing publication, wrote about anti-Semitism here in a way that practically made Paris sound like Berlin on Kristallnacht; *The Washington Post* has featured a steady drumbeat of francophobic columnists; *The Atlantic Monthly* published a blurb linking Chirac and Osama. That kind of vituperative, hateful France-bashing has certainly not been reciprocated in France.

Here's how one simpleton—that would be me—sees the three instances of what Wells cites as our media's "virulent" France-bashing :

■ According to its own government, France is witnessing more anti-Semitic crimes than at any time since the French government privatized anti-Semitism by getting out of the business itself in 1944. Meanwhile, Wells' employer, the *New York Times,* reported in 2002 that the dramatic increase in anti-Semitism has been "the worst spate of anti-Jewish violence in France since World War II"—and it's grown much worse since. Anti-Semitism in France is unparalleled in Europe—it's one of the few things that the French are better at than the rest of the European Union—with numbers ballooning so fast now that hardly a week goes by without a synagogue or two being torched or a Jewish cemetery vandalized or a Jewish kid getting beaten or killed for no reason other than the fact that he's Jewish. Anti-Semitism may be something far too exotic, perhaps, for Walter Wells' social circle to notice, especially since his circle weighs everything against the alleged suffering of the Palestinians, who are the victims of chic choice, and dismisses blatant anti-Semitism as fantasy in comparison. French fascists may be less obvious than others, but one wonders exactly how bad it has to get before Francophiles like Wells take it as seriously as all those "virulent" editors at *Vanity Fair* did when they reported on the phenomenon.

■ The *Washington Post*'s mostly liberal columnists have indeed taken France to task over one thing or another, I suppose, but Wells doesn't offer any examples of blatant American hatred of France (which is what I assume he means when he speaks of "francophobia," since it's obvious he couldn't mean "fear of France"). The closest I could come to finding an actual instance of this sort of Francophobia was in February 2003, when Richard Cohen accused Dennis Kucinich of having studied his logic in France, something he did only after Kucinich claimed on *Meet the Press* that getting Iraq's oil was the only case that the Bush administration had made for war. (When Richard Perle called Kucinich a liar, Cohen reported that Kucinich "roared back, 'Well, if America is not at threat, then what is this about? And many people are wondering: "How did our oil get under their sand?"'" Cohen wondered, "How did this fool get on 'Meet the Press'?")

■ As for the *Atlantic* publishing a blurb linking Chirac and Osama, how "vituperative and hateful" is this? "What do Osama bin Laden and Jacques Chirac have in common? In a recent Pew Research Center sampling of post–Iraq War attitudes around the world, a majority of Jordanians expressed confidence in both men's ability 'to do the right thing.'" This is "vituperative, hateful France-bashing"?

Now, when I'm sitting around reading the *New York Post* in my Appalachian doublewide, I'm just a beer-swilling devotee (if you'll pardon my French) of FOX News who thinks that people who eat snails are *different*.

But the reason I have taken a moment to focus on Mr. Wells is because his sentiments mirror exactly those of the French elite: The slightest hint of disapproval is seen by everybody from the mayor of a small Picardy village right on down to Chirac as "vituperative, hateful France-bashing." For the record, French history bashes France. Those of us who dislike France simply read the record and call the blow-by-blow.

Besides, the French bash back just fine. In *Le Monde*, anti-Americanism is as pervasive as it is in the elite French circle that provides the paper with its modest and shrinking readership; Bush has been portrayed as a Hitler, America as a killer state and so on. The tenor, if not the texture, of *Le Monde* is redolent of the patchouli press of the Sixties. A typical *Le Monde* editorial cartoon shows a hulking American soldier in full combat gear stomping lethally over piles of sweet-faced little children and complaining, "This sandstorm is terrible!" It isn't Yank-bashing, of course. It's all good fun. (And it's not limited to *Le Monde;* every French paper has its go at America, and so do those who work in the German press, to whom America is "brutal" and worse. It's also not something that began with George W. Bush; the United States was just as despised by the French elite five, ten, thirty, sixty years ago. During Reagan's administration, anti-Americanism was especially brutal.)

But as it happens, the ringmaster of *Le Monde*, Jean-Marie Colombani—once seen as a respectable, if heavily biased, editor—is becoming more famous in Paris as just another corrupt journalist. Two leading French investigative reporters, Pierre Péan and Philippe Cohen (in a best-selling book called *La face cachée du Monde*), have accused Colombani of siphoning off a million francs (about $150,000) as a "commission" for funds the paper received as a subsidy from the French government. Colombani was only stopped by threat of disclosure. He was also accused of using the paper's editorial columns to gain advantage in business deals. *Le Monde*, the two men wrote, was a "modern-day Pravda" governed by Colombani and two underlings, editor in chief Edwy Plenel and board chairman Alain Minc, in a "climate of fear."

French journalist Airy Routier, reviewing *La face cachée du Monde*, claimed that after Colombani and his draconian henchmen "had cleverly modified the corporate bylaws to seal their power, *Le Monde* was transformed into a lawless, almost Mafialike enterprise that used blackmail and influence peddling in a style reminiscent of France's corrupt financial newspapers of the pre–World War II era." Colombani tried to sue Péan and Cohen, but had to back off. When Daniel Schneidermann, a respected television interviewer and a veteran editorialist for the paper, wrote a book that mentioned the Péan-Cohen book and criticized Colombani's reaction to it, he was fired.

Today, Plenel has resigned and *Le Monde* is in serious financial trouble, with its own staff reporting that the paper is out of touch with its readers almost as much as its readers are out of touch with reality. As in America, people who want serious news stripped of ideology are finding it easy to go elsewhere. The propaganda tool that De Gaulle hoped would give credibility to his nationalistic myth is losing readers to the Internet and to other afternoon papers, as well as to its traditional rivals, *Le Figaro* and *Libération*.

6.

It is time to stop pretending that Europeans and Americans share a common view of the world, or even that they occupy the same world. On the all-important question of power—the efficacy of power, the morality of power, the desirability of power—American and European perspectives are diverging. Europe is turning

away from power, or to put it a little differently, it is moving beyond power into a self-contained world of laws and rules and transnational negotiation and cooperation. It is entering a post-historical paradise of peace and relative prosperity, the realization of Kant's "Perpetual Peace." The United States, meanwhile, remains mired in history, exercising power in the anarchic Hobbesian world where international laws and rules are unreliable and where true security and the defense and promotion of a liberal order still depend on the possession and use of military might. That is why on major strategic and international questions today, Americans are from Mars and Europeans are from Venus: They agree on little and understand one another less and less. And this state of affairs is not transitory—the product of one American election or one catastrophic event. The reasons for the transatlantic divide are deep, long in development, and likely to endure. When it comes to setting national priorities, determining threats, defining challenges, and fashioning and implementing foreign and defense policies, the United States and Europe have parted ways.
—Robert Kagan, *Policy Review*, June 2002

... the problem of terror is one that is underlying the whole [Israeli-Palestinian] problem and makes discussion very difficult and it is clearly the sine qua non is to try to deal with the terror problem here, but at the same time, it's important to create a climate that allows for the confidence to be rebuilt, which is why I called for time-out on acts that are regarded by each side as provocative.
—U.S. Secretary of State Madeline Albright to NBC's Andrea Mitchell, September 1997

IRAQ HAS PROVIDED THE FRENCH PRESS with a predictably easy context for its habitual animosity toward America. And they have plenty of company. In Iraq, where Tet is around every corner, the French view of America is part of almost every journalist's perspective. I don't know if I can pretend that all the lousy journalism that's come out of Iraq is the fault of the French, so let's do this, instead: Let's just say that all the journalists in Iraq *are* French, at least metaphysically speaking.

The conceit isn't totally bizarre. The war in Iraq is the first major conflict of the twenty-first century and comes at a time when the widespread education of women that took place in the second half of the twentieth century has finally had a defining impact not just on private and social-sexual dynamics but also on the androgynous culture that has arisen as a result of such a massive demographic warp. The world has changed since 1945. Today we live in a heavily feminized culture. Every night is ladies' night in America. Just turn on the TV and see for yourself.

No matter what progressive social engineers might wish, men are different from women and conflict between the sexes predictably has resulted in friction. This has been described profitably by John (*Men Are from Mars, Women Are from Venus*) Gray, and repurposed by Robert Kagan to explain the divergence of American and European worldviews. But the formula also applies to other more or less parallel cohorts, as the following helpful chart shows.

Mars	Venus
Jack Daniel's	Muscadet
Rugby	Synchronized swimming
Mel Gibson	Michael Moore
Steak	Tofu
Field & Stream	*Metropolitan Home*
Chevy Suburban	Toyota Prius
Swift boat vets	Dan Rather and CBS
Viagra	Prozac
Bill O'Reilly	John Stewart
South Park	*The West Wing*
FX	Lifetime
Guantanamo	Time-outs

The American and the European media are for the most part *très* French and straight from Venus. Compared with Martians like George W. Bush or Donald Rumsfeld or the vast majority of the population of the United States, who distrust journalists more than used-car salesmen, the press is wildly liberal, feminized when they're not outright feminine, pacifistic, self-obsessed, vain, hysterical, desperate to be *fabulous* to their friends, cliquish, happy to bend the rules to accommodate sentiment, prone to inventing excuses for bad behavior and very often indulging in it themselves—maybe out of empathy.

Wars against terrorism are strictly Marsville. The Venus people believe that the way you fight a war against terrorism is to give the combatants a "time-out" because that's how they saw a conflict being resolved in their children's preschool that time they accidentally stopped by early. As a result, we now fight apologetic, feminized wars, like the one in Iraq—wars that can't be won, because on the soft, Venusian landscape there should be no ugly winners; winning is unkind and insensitive and aggressive, and people who need to win are not very interested in consensus. And by all means, there should be no losers. So in Iraq, Mars attacked, Venus went into hysterics, and the entire press corps went directly to France.

The ultimate rearview vindication of this perspective is, you guessed it, Vietnam. Venus-charmed, Frenchified journalists love the Vietnam analogy because it refers to a war that America lost. (The French lost a war there, too, but it was long ago, plus they're *French*.) The Vietnam analogy is one the French have used to describe every American military adventure since Vietnam. Every time a GI raises a rifle and points toward a target, no matter how small, the Frenchified press raises the specter of Vietnam. Grenada was Vietnam. Panama? Vietnam. Afghanistan was Vietnam times two. It is the wisdom of the press that there is no wisdom save common wisdom. And the common wisdom during the first year and a half after the ouster of Saddam was that Iraq was Vietnam. Even Michael Moore said so.

Only five months after the Iraq invasion, Richard Cohen, that France-bashing *Washington Post* columnist, famously did a Nexis survey that showed "more than 800 links" in a single week "where the words 'Iraq' and 'Vietnam' appeared together" in the same news story as an analogy, implied or otherwise. Sandy Berger, the former national security advisor to President Bill Clinton who cushions his instep with classified documents he accidentally steals from the government, called the situation a "classic guerrilla war." French and British newspapers sported headlines right out of '68. "Rebel war spirals out of control as U.S. intelligence loses the plot," headlined the *Observer*.

Often, the U.S. press hands the French press useful ammo. For example, the appearance in *USA Today* of a memo written by Donald Rumsfeld saying that winning the peace in Iraq would be a "long, hard slog" gave the French press great comfort. The French Communist daily *l'Humanité* reported that the intensity of the guerrilla activity against Coalition forces was compelling senators, congressmen and members of the administration to see in Iraq a "parallel with Vietnam" and that "Washington [was] in turmoil" because what the paper called a lie used by the United States to go to war against Iraq had been revealed. Every day, said the paper, the murderous attacks lead America deeper into an "inextricable conflict," one that is "catastrophic and dangerous" and a "very long way today from the initial objective: 'freedom for Iraq'." *Le Nouvel Observateur* reported signs of political collapse. The naïve U.S. military gave a crew from TF1, a popular French channel, access to the patients at the U.S. military hospital at Ramstein AFB, in southwestern Germany. The result was ten minutes of agitprop, in which interviews were harvested from amputees and otherwise traumatized American GIs wounded in Iraq. One guy had to explain how he thought he was carrying his buddy out of harm's way during a firefight—then discovered that he was rescuing only part of his friend. The camera pulled in tight on the poor man's deadened eyes. No tears. The inescapable message: This is the face of failure. *Le Parisien* showed George W. Bush confronting more "disastrous news" coming from Iraq, while *Le Point* reported that more and more Americans were wondering whether or not Iraq was becoming another Vietnam, citing a *Washington Post* story suggesting that the escalation of violence in Iraq might create the same shift away from public support of the war that took place in the United States after media coverage of the Tet Offensive in 1968 convinced Americans that the effort in Vietnam was a lost cause.

It was a reasonable assertion: First of all, every French journalist already knows it is. And second, so do most American reporters, as Cohen's survey demonstrated.

Actually, within a few days of the invasion, it had already become all quagmire all the time in the press. In the ongoing media remake of *The Four Feathers* that played out in newsrooms across Europe, it fell to the *Daily Telegraph*'s venerable military analyst, John Keegan, to play the role of General Burroughs, the old guy who keeps explaining to the young Favershams of Fleet Street the facts of military life: "The older media generation, particularly those covering the war from comfortable television studios," Keegan wrote after the first month of the war, "has not covered itself with glory. Deeply infected with anti-war feeling and Left-wing antipathy to the use of force as a means of doing good, it has once again sought to depict the achievements of the West's servicemen as a subject for disapproval.... The brave young American and British servicemen—and women—who have risked their lives to bring down Saddam have every reason to feel that there is something corrupt about their home-based media."

Describing the coverage of the initial stages of the war, Keegan wrote, "You wouldn't know it from reading the daily dispatches, but this has been a collapse, not a war." If only the French had known! All across that garlic-scented land, *les citoyens* were slapping themselves on the forehead and saying, "*Zut!* Collapses are us!"

By then it was too late to rush for some booty, so the Parisian press and the rest all settled into the after-war and the chance to document the losing of the peace. By then, Saddamite terrorists and crazy zealots had already become "militants"—like, say, Erin Brockovich?—or "resistance fighters"—very much like France's own, no doubt. And the media was in the way, all the way. British TV broadcast a documentary showing two heroic women from an

American newspaper in-country on their first big assignment. The camera followed them as they followed the troops. When a body was found on a street, they were joined by dozens of other hacks who swooped in from nowhere and swarmed over the body like giant flies, shutters snapping away. At another stop, where a child was being buried, the photographer jumped out of the car, ran to the burial site, pushed the grieving mother out of the way and took her snapshot of a dead baby that she already knew would never run in a family newspaper. "I hated to push her like that," she said, approximately, "but it was the picture of a career." Was it ever.

Virtually all the reporting from Iraq was the same stuff we were shoveled from Vietnam: sentimental, context-free, anecdotal claptrap substituting for informed insight. In war reporting, everybody wants to write first-person features under fire. But for every John Burns, the *New York Times'* man who really does work hard at getting it right, there are a hundred journalists playing Scoop at the hotel bar asking each other what the story is, fearful of reporting against received wisdom, looking for the dead baby and the picture of a career.

It may have been that the level of violence in Iraq was microscopic compared with what happened in Vietnam, and maybe the geopolitical details didn't quite line up with all those Southeast Asian dominos. But so what? To build a case, you have to start someplace, yes? After all, in the European and American press, Vietnam was the *only* way to understand and report Iraq. Certainly the Iraqi terrorists knew that, with their almost-every-Sunday atrocity driving the weekly news cycle. Because of a combination of media-inspired public animosity and absurd, poll-driven policy decisions, we lost in Vietnam, America's first apologetic war. Therefore, unless we do something radically different, we will lose in Iraq. It's, like, fate.

What history can teach us is that cheesy French-style reporting, stripped of history and understanding but rich in arrogance and sentimentality, leads to lost wars and Cambodia-sized body counts. Walter Cronkite still stands, Walter Duranty-like, behind his absurd Tet Offensive broadcast in 1968, a piece of work that gave credence to all the crisis-jive reported before him by other, even worse journos, and set a precedent that certainly hasn't served CBS or the media well since. Thanks to more reasonable journalists, such as the late Robert Bartley, who visited the topic of Tet in the *Wall Street Journal* ("The truth about the Tet offensive is that we won . . . ."), and Peter Braestrup, whose classic *Big Story* is the definitive study of media malpractice during and after Tet, we now know how lousy the journalism coming from Vietnam really was—and how pathetic journalists are who try to defend it and pretend the truth never happened. All that journalists in Iraq know about covering wars they learned from watching their elders cover the war in Vietnam. The formulations are cozy and comforting: over-armed Americans stumbling from one manslaughter to another, a fragile folk culture under attack, weeping women, etc. So, in the only way that makes sense to the press, Iraq *is* Vietnam.

Maybe it's time we finally learned our lesson. Let's bring them all home—the journalists, that is. Western journalists feminized the war and reduced it to a series of sobbing anecdotes, while real women—the ones who served in Iraq in the Coalition forces—were doing the tough work. We're better off sending women to war and keeping the journalists home, barefoot and tied to their Valium, where they won't get hurt. If it's necessary, we can always devise a smarter set of policies for Iraq. But no matter what, we're never going to be able to build a smarter press corps.

Is this censorship? *Mais oui!* Fortunately, Cronkite's on my side in this one. "I'm for censorship," Cronkite told the News World International Conference in Dublin in October 2003. He pointed out that during World War II, all dispatches were vetted by the military. Despite that, democracy survived. But maybe it was because of that.

After thirty-five years, it's about time Walter was right about something. Bring the press back home. Keep the children of Venus out of the way of the lads from Mars. License them, maybe. Make them take a written exam or something. Send them up to Paris to stand in line a couple of years for a permit.

All's fair in love and war. If Michael Jackson can keep the media out of Neverland, then surely the United States should be able to keep the media out of Iraq.

7.

MAYBE WE COULD LEARN a thing or two about getting along with the French and the British—if we could just get them to sober up. In a startling moment of clarity—the kind of painful moment that follows a night of binge drinking, no doubt—the British were *shocked* to discover recently that they had a drinking problem. On weekend nights, drunks take to the streets and fall down in them. They fight, hurl and pass out in gutters.

It became such a problem that in early spring 2004, the government decided to try to convince drinkers to become more French in their drinking habits. We want a "continental café-bar culture," a Labour minister said, pronouncing the word "culture" as "co-cha." But for some reason, the punters wouldn't take to sipping Fernet-Branca and discussing Sartre, and soon the UK press, where drinking is rarely a problem, became concerned: What could possibly cause such a thing? they asked. Is it a sign of rising despair? Or is it a symptom of declining morality?

Neither. The British spirits industry was convinced that commercials were persuading otherwise innocent Britons to drink bingefully and with intent. The Portman Group, which, the papers say, is "the body set up by the alcohol industry to campaign for sensible drinking"—like a giant stuffed vicar sitting at a bar in Gloucestershire, I guess—issued a report complaining that "the standards applied to drinks advertising [have] become so relaxed that many TV ads are breaking industry-wide rules." The report cited a couple of vodka manufacturers who were guilty of "associating their products with sexual performance through packaging and branding." *Packaging and branding?* The code also prohibits "scenes showing drinks being consumed quickly."

Now, as it happens, one of the many career potholes along this thoroughfare of woe I call a life was my employment as a barman in London. My job was to pour pints all evening, then sing cowboy songs at closing time. The landlord, Michael Smith, discovered that my rendition of "Git Along, Little Doggies" cleared the place of drunks much, much faster than his shouts of "Time, please!" Nothing else was quite so conducive to producing a scene showing drinks being consumed quickly as my semi-yodel.

I am therefore an expert on irresponsible drinking, yet even though the British government has created an "alcohol harm reduction strategy" to contain the problem—which costs the UK some $37 billion per year—I have heard from *no one* seeking my sober wisdom. Too bad, because my solution is simple and cheap: Since binge drinking suggests drinking to excess at occasional intervals, the government should run commercials encouraging a more or less consistent level of drunkenness.

Instead, the British are simply staggering away from the problem—a solution with unintended benefits. Recently, the *Daily Telegraph* ran a series of stories, the scoop of which was that Brits have "had enough of life in Britain." Slowly, methodically, they are leaving the UK, and they are invading and conquering their two fiercest and most ancient of foes. That would be France and Spain, where the British are engaging in binge property acquisition. The phenomenon is now so ubiquitous that the BBC has a whole reality TV series based on what happens when a family of, say, working-class yobs leave their ancestral home in a blighted suburb of, say, Leeds and wash up in Torremolinos, where they try to realize their lifelong dream of, say, opening a bar, having closed so many over the years.

With nearly a million UK expats already on the ground there and elsewhere, victory over the French and the Spanish must be nigh. Just to make sure, reinforcements are on the way! Some twenty million more people are thinking of bailing out of Britain. The *Daily Telegraph* editorialized to warn against such foolishness, neatly listing all the reasons why any sensible person would want to stay in Old Blighty: "... a climate that offers us a bit of everything (but nothing too extreme); the best foreign restaurants in the world; country pubs; the Queen; plenty to grouse about; a tradition of tolerance; The Daily Telegraph; freedom of a sort; and even the ability to pop frequently over the Channel, safe in the knowledge that we can easily return." Some list. No BBC. No Church of England. No National Health Service. No binge drinking!

The Spaniards, not surprisingly, seem delighted to make a little business selling Marmite and condos to pasty people in loose shorts and black shoes.

But in mirthless France, the British are breeding nothing but melancholy resentment. It seems *les Anglais* have arrived in bulk, purchased huge chunks of grim Brittany and, as the *Telegraph* reported, are now making life hard for the indigenous peoples. " 'The problem is they are pushing up property prices and we locals just can't keep up,' said Gaston, 37, amid sips of a morning beer."

In my neck of France, so many properties are being shopped by Brits that local realtors have added English-speaking agents to help explain the charms of ramshackle farmhouses made of sticks and mud to English gentlefolk from Kent. Sometimes, there are misunderstandings. Take, for example, the poor middle-aged woman from London who bought a bar on a corner of the battlefield at Agincourt.

According to her friends, it was a setup. They told me that after suffering the death of her child, and in deep despair, she had been lured there by an evil cousin who, in cahoots with the local mayor, told her all about the thousands of Britons who visit the place every year to commemorate one of England's most memorable victories over the French, when Henry V's small but heroic band of English archers, outnumbered five to one and suffering from diarrhea so bad they fought without their pants on, defeated the flower of French aristocracy under crazy Charles VI on St. Crispin's Day in 1415. It's the sort of thing to which any self-respecting Englishman might like to raise a toast.

Trouble is, the only drinking place in that part of France is indelibly French.

So the woman sold everything she owned, then added it to a small inheritance she had recently gained, moved to Agincourt and bought the café. Financially, she was clueless; linguistically, she was Frenchless. According to her friends, she was systematically milked of every last penny by unscrupulous locals who took advantage of her naïveté—to use her only French word—to add to her bills such a sum that she would never be able to pay it off. And sure enough, when that happened she was then abandoned by everyone she trusted, including her husband, and sent back to London in poverty and tears. The café was subsequently resold by the mayor to a British school and it's now being used as a study center. The new director is a very charming Englishwoman. So in the second Battle of Agincourt, the French may have prevailed— but only temporarily. Teetotalers won the war.

But that victory will be as meaningless to France as Henry's was to England. What good does it do to win back one café for a few months when the English are occupying huge tracts of Pas de Calais, crowding the restaurants, driving up the property values, careering down the roads in their left-hand-drive autos and taking over the villages in the famous Sept Vallées? I'm certain there are now more Britons living in France than at any time in the last four hundred years. Some French villages, I'm told, are now almost entirely British. One has an English mayor. Writers and artists are once again bolting to the Continent; Theodore Dalrymple recently told his *Spectator* readers that he too was joining the Chunnel exodus in search of a higher civilization. Whole boatloads of Brits are bringing their famous brown teeth to France for a bit of dentistry because British dentists are bad and overbooked. Earlier this year, a retired Londoner gave me tea in his garden in Tramecourt and said, "I love it here. It reminds me of the England of my youth."

8.

ANOTHER THING ABOUT FRANCE that generates fondness in the heart of an American leftist is the fact that in France, as elsewhere in Europe, there's a Green Party, the organized political gesture of all those who are oppressed by Nike and McDonald's and who yearn for a cleaner planet free of global capitalism, but with cheaper laptops.

In Europe, manifestations of Green romanticism are all around, not just in the list of parties that clutter the ballots in France, Germany, Italy and elsewhere. For example, there's a widespread, irrational fear in Europe of genetically modified food, the kind of stuff that has been used to feed emaciated, sickly Americans for years, and the kind of agricultural product that could help eliminate Third World hunger in a rainy season or two.

But in the European Union, at the top of the special-interest food chain is, well, food. The EU's Common Agricultural Policy—which was invented as a way to swap French agricultural products for German machinery, with little regard for the effects it had on other nations—allows my neighbors in this little French farming village to drive tractors that make Escalades look like Fiats.

The CAP was born in a 1962 agreement between De Gaulle and Germany's Konrad Adenauer, part of the web of entangling alliances that bound two crippled economies together in an effort to give them both at least one leg to stand on. It also established an early model for all subsequent EU treaties, in that its primary purpose was to use all of Europe as a means of propping up its two largest states—that would be France and Germany. It involved heavy community-funded supports for French farmers and a tariff protecting them from barbarian imports. These days, the CAP exists largely to keep French farmers out of downtown Paris, which is where they go, smelly manure spreaders in tow, whenever anybody threatens to cut their subsidies or remove their longstanding trade protections. The impending importation of "genetically modified organisms"—part of the American master plan for world domination, according to alarmist articles in *Le Monde* and elsewhere—poses a very real and considerable health threat to French politicians not only because of the impact it may have on French agriculture, but because of what it means for France generally.

As an example of the kind of EU-enhanced quid pro quo that provides a European tit for a French tat, the CAP can't be beat. The threat comes from America, naturally—in this case in the form of GMOs like those growing in the middle of a small cornfield in a corner of Pas de Calais, where in June 2003 I not very accidentally came across a lanky farmer committing illegal agriculture on the perilous edge of biotechnology.

He was growing corn, the genetically modified variety imported from the United States. "The stuff's *fantastic,*" he said, explaining that GM corn not only grows quicker than he expected, but also is resistant to the kind of pests that nearly led him to a corn-free summer the previous year. "I wanted to see what would happen, and now I know." He told me he had discovered "the master race of corn."

Of course, Nazi jokes are ten Euro-cents a metric dozen in France. But in this case, one man's genetic masterpiece is another's scary special effect, in which an ear of pest-resistant corn becomes a skull and crossbones and the symbol of grasping globalization, which is the new manifestation of the kind of political romanticism that used to engender folk songs about Uncle Joe Stalin.

So, at the same time the man in northern France was crowing over his alien corn, in another part of France, in a prison in Millau in the hot, hot south, sat José Bové, who likes to call himself a sheep farmer. But José Bové, with his droopy mustache and briar pipe, is actually a professional poster boy—the David Hasselhof of modern French anticapitalism. He's a shepherd the same way Al Sharpton is a clergyman. José Bové's flock is the herd of

French journalists who follow him everywhere and who have made him the star of the French Birkenstock movement.

Bové, who spent four years at Berkeley, where his parents worked as researchers, is very much a typical left-wing media creature. He travels the world to campuses and demos and meetings wrapped in the colors of his radical French farmers' union; recently, he showed up to chat with Yasser Arafat, looking angry but rural. A typical leftist anti-Semite, Bové believes that anti-Semitic acts in France are the work of the Israeli intelligence service trying to make France look bad. Or worse. He gets money from ... *someplace.* He earned the respect of the Republic of France by wielding a chainsaw and leading a mob that attacked the McDonald's in Millau and tore the place apart. Just think what Delacroix could have done with that!

■ ■ ■ ■ ■

FRANCE DOES HAVE some problems that might inspire action on the part of those who are friends of the earth and all the animals that dwell upon it. In fact, to locate an interesting Green dilemma, you can play it like spin-the-bottle: You choose one of the spokes that go out of Paris, out of the big city like all other big cities, out into the countryside. The direction you end up going says a lot about what sort of person you get to be, at least for the moment. Hedonist? Head south, where the beaches are jammed with people and holiday litter. Humorless and wiry? Go for the Alps, where it's a rare mountainside that doesn't have a ski slope carved into its side somewhere. Personally, I'm pulled north and west, back toward places more familiar, for various reasons, like England and Belgium, places I know well and love for their predictability.

But heading north, the prism of French existence, with its equivocations and exceptions and eccentricities, intrudes all along the way, past country-western restaurants and roadside cafés named after crazy kings, until, in the Pas de Calais, on a bright Easter morning, it finds perfect expression in the gaily dressed parishioners filing out of an old stone church in a village surrounded by gentle fields sloping up toward distant, sun-drenched hills. They linger in the graveyard, old people, new flowers, young children, all slowly making their way to the church hall, which was new in the late 1950s, I guess.

We were invited in to "see the roosters"—and I readily agreed because, as a gentleman from rural Pennsylvania, I thought a display of the varieties of local poultry would be an interesting addition to my three young daughters' agricultural experiences.

Inside, genial men offered wine for a euro a cup and a ticket seller charged a pittance for admission. But the parallel 4-H universe dropped away once we got into the hall, where a miniature boxing ring had been erected in the center of the smoky room. Roosters from every nearby village and town were being brought in, some arriving in impressively decorated crates. Folding chairs were crammed into a circle surrounding the ring. An apparently feeble man in a wheelchair was guided in, seats were moved, and an aisle materialized until he was pushed to ringside. He nodded softly, a cigarette dangling from his lips, and appeared to doze. The first pair of roosters was brought into the ring and released, their spurs augmented by silver blades, a practice frowned on in more civilized countries—like Iraq, for example. (I looked it up later online. When a Reuters reporter asked Faris al Qaisey, owner of The Ancient Casino of Baghdad, the capital's most popular cockfighting venue, what he thought of giving weapons to roosters, he said, "This is an Islamic state. We would not do that." France is merely 15 percent Islamic, so restraint will have to wait.)

When the roosters were let loose, the old man in the wheelchair immediately came to life and began crowing, shouting the names of the village associated with each rooster, giving odds and calling out for bets. The men—and a few women—in the crowd called back, even as the roosters fought. He kept it all in his head, nodding, pointing, shouting, while a stove timer ticked away. Even before the regulation five minutes, it was all over—one rooster sat on another, both motionless and apparently unharmed. Nevertheless, my wife and the girls were out the door before the first feather flew, warned by a well-dressed young woman who had come home from Paris for Easter that it might be good to scoot the chairs back a little to avoid blood stains. I stayed on through three more nearly bloodless matches. It was like watching beetles argue.

Cockfighting is theoretically illegal in France. And France was the last signatory, in 1999, to the EU's Treaty of Amsterdam, Protocol 10 of which is intended to "ensure improved protection and respect for the welfare of animals as sentient beings." But the provision makes exceptions for things like regional traditions, and in these rural precincts, where cockfighting has been enjoyed through all five of the French republics, the traditional matches are well publicized and the communities who host them are enthusiastic. "The old men like them," the girl from Paris had said. But the hall was filled with young families and women, all snacking and sipping from plastic cups. Evidence of cockfighting fandom is everywhere in the northern reaches of Pas de Calais. At an old, atmospheric café in Aire, a collection of trophies sits behind the bar, a golden fowl perched atop each one. By early evening, men start drifting in, boxes in hand. A pair of doors in the back opens, and for a moment you can see inside the gloomy, shuttered room. An arena has been fashioned out of old planks, a cockpit in the center. You see the trophies everywhere after that—at sports bars, family restaurants, quiet cafés in tiny towns. Cockfighting is the guilty pleasure of the blue-collar north, like pro wrestling with duller plumage.

■ ■ ■ ■ ■

BUT COCKFIGHTING ISN'T SOMETHING that ignites the sanctimonious fuse of somebody like José Bové. The thing that gets him is "genetically modified organisms" or GMOs. Like others on the

French left, he sees GMOs as yet another example of probably lethal American treachery, worse even than a McDonald's. For a long time, Bové and his followers have been vandalizing the property of others in an effort to outlaw agricultural innovations. When brought before a judge, he patiently explains that he's a one-man legislature: "Yes, this action was illegal, but I lay claim to it because it was legitimate," he informed a court in 1998.

In 1998 and again in 1999, Bové broke into a lab, destroyed scientific records, trashed a bunch of GM seeds and tore up crops. He was arrested, tried and found guilty in November 2002 and sentenced to ten months in the pokey—a politically unhealthy sentence which the government conspired to have judicially modified. Bové, who understood press pimping rather well, refused. Instead, he returned to his farm and waited for the government to back down rather than face the wrath of his supporters. More than six months later, on June 22, 2003, the police arrived at Bové's farm at dawn, nabbed him from his bed, tossed him in a helicopter and flew him directly to the jail at Villeneuve-lès-Maguelone. The French press was outraged. Bové's lawyer condemned the arrest as a French "commando operation," despite the fact that it was successful. Around the world, small demonstrations were held outside French consulates where organizers, such as Food First in San Francisco, explained that "Bové's actions are a symbolic protest against the current system, in which transnational agribusiness and biotechnology corporations are given legal sanction and economic assistance by governments to dump cheap, genetically modified food onto markets"—because as everyone knows, the poor hate to eat and would prefer to buy expensive organic food.

It was nonsense, and really just another salvo in the ongoing U.S.-French war over genetically modified organisms. At about the time of the Bové arrest, *Libération* reported that George W. Bush had launched a "diatribe" on the subject of GMOs on the eve of an EU-U.S. meeting in Washington. To an American, the idea of a George W. Bush "diatribe" suggests a mastery of language unfamiliar to most of us. But to Bové and his supporters in the French government, genetically modified food = Yankee death chow, the culinary equivalent of smallpox in blankets, exactly the kind of trick that W would use to raise money for Halliburton or something like that.

So while they puff their Gauloises and tailgate like madmen, the French, who couldn't even be persuaded that *potatoes* were safe to eat until the late eighteenth century, and who until the 1930s thought dogs brought to the New World would stop barking because of the pitiful hygiene of the place, insisted on trying to maintain the European Union's policy of keeping GMOs out of Europe—a policy that comforts Green weenies, but kills people in places like Africa, where the crops could feed the hungry, but where governments won't accept genetically modified seed because the EU restrictions would mean they couldn't export back to Europe the surplus food that would result from the improved harvest. Not incidentally, an anti-GMO policy also means more support for French agriculture, something not lost on Chirac as he continues to skirt efforts to reform France's CAP, and a lovely skirt it is, too.

Within twenty-four hours of his arrest, Bové had become the celebrity that the French union movement so desperately needed. After a season of electoral disasters, and after all those soporific semi-strikes in opposition to government entitlements reform, the left needed somebody to celebrate—so *way*, José. Green Party officials pointed out that Bové was being treated like a . . . a prisoner! The French media jumped on the story like a Johnny Halliday divorce. And the whole thing went instantly French: unions promptly rallied to Bové's cause; a mob was mobilized; angry demonstrators set fire to a *hedge*. What's that about, anyway?

Finally, *Le Monde* revealed that Bové was asking for the ultimate French honor: He wished to be transfigured into a character from Dumas and declared a political prisoner, a legal status that would ease the discomfort of his circumstance and sanctify his martyrdom. He'd also be able to raise more money and attract more visitors, among other things. One gift idea? An organic hacksaw stuffed into a Big Mac. Chirac turned him down, but used his Bastille Day pardon powers to reduce Bové's sentence to six months so all those sheep of his wouldn't suffer.

■ ■ ■ ■ ■

WHEN THE HARDWORKING antiglobalists of France aren't campaigning for more expensive food, they're working to enshrine the Kyoto Protocol, a plan to drain the economies of developed countries in an effort to make sure that greenhouse gasses, the presumed cause of the apparent climate shift, all come from the Third World.

Like the European Union itself, Kyoto is part of the wardrobe of rectitude in which cynical French politicians drape themselves. America, because the president and the Senate (without dissent) both roundly rejected the treaty, gets to play the environmental bad guy in this little charade. The United States has continued to find Kyoto to be unworkable and, most of all, expensive.

Critics have futilely documented the flaws in Kyoto to undisturbed liberals—as Danish researcher Bjorn Lomborg did for readers of the *Guardian* recently, when he wrote that "for the same amount implementing Kyoto will cost the EU every year, the UN estimates that we could provide every person in the world with access to basic health, education, family planning and water and sanitation services." Although George W. Bush—the right-wing president who made Arlen Specter senator-for-life, embraced affirmative action, etched Title IX in stone, inflated the Department of Education like a liberal love-doll, but finally stood up for his principles by not inviting Ted Kennedy over to the house for movies and popcorn anymore—had developed his own pathetically articulated environmental policy, one that took economic realities into account and balanced them against semi-scientific theories, it didn't really matter. The U.S. refusal to sign the Kyoto agreement gave hypocritical politicians in France the opportunity to harness yet another mule to their anti-American bandwagon.

Truth be told, there's not a globally warmed snowball's chance in south Miami that France, or the rest of the EU, will be able to meet its own commitment under the Kyoto agreement to reduce its greenhouse gas emissions by 8 percent from 1990 levels. In 2004, the EU announced that for all practical purposes, compliance with Kyoto was far, far away.

That isn't a revelation to those who have been driving policy in Yank-bashing EU states; they knew all along that Kyoto, like the stability pact, may have been a nice idea, but one on which they were never going to risk political capital. If they had to choose some lovely Green fantasy over political survival, the choice would be an easy one. Germany is the EU's biggest greenhouse gasser, and one of the states that made a huge, early stride toward meeting its commitment to Kyoto—mostly by simply closing down all those fume-spewing East German Trabant factories once the Wall came down.

But now the money crunch is on and, as the *Suddeutsche Zeitung* recently headlined, *"Kyoto im Koma."* Just as they failed to meet their economic stability pact commitments, Germany and France are both falling behind their Kyoto targets, a failure that will increase as long as environmental whimsy remains a luxury, and the rest of the EU is following suit. My bet: If you asked Chirac whether he'd rather have palm trees growing in Normandy or an unemployment check, he'd take the coconuts on Omaha Beach.

But that will not stop the French from demanding that the United States sign on for industrial poverty, especially now that Russia has joined Kyoto's lemming brigade. An American signature on Kyoto would be just one more way the French could insist that the United States meet its multilateral obligations by becoming poorer. For America to do that is fair. For France to do that is unthinkable.

For more than two centuries, that kind of tax-the-rich, obsessively jealous mentality has characterized the "friendship" that France feels toward the United States. Maybe it's time America played swat-the-fly and demanded to know just who the hell the French think they are, anyway.

Who they are, of course, is the enemy.

the enemy

I ONCE SPENT A BIRTHDAY in an Egyptian holding pen surrounded by eighty-eight men in burnouses—mostly Libyans, I think—and a guy who looked a little like a guy I once knew in California. This was all long ago, my dear lads, so long ago that I actually noticed birthdays.

I had returned from Sudan, where I was doing some reporting on a giant engineering project in the southern part of the country, way up the Nile, where the Egyptian government was involved in a plan to drain a swamp the size of Connecticut in order to regulate the flow of the great river more effectively—and thus boost Egyptian agriculture and commerce. Egyptian meddling in Sudan could have had a destabilizing effect on the Sudanese government of the day, which was a relatively moderate one, so the project was sensitive. I presume that's why I was "quarantined" for a few days while my possessions were detained elsewhere.

The prison wasn't Mazra'at Tora, the notorious main jail just outside Cairo. It was the universally despised medical quarantine station, a hot and dusty concrete detention center tucked behind Cairo's airport. Instead of the brutality of Mazra'at Tora, at the *quarantina* you were battered by boredom and what paradoxically seemed to be bureaucratic indifference. Ostensibly used to segregate travelers entering Egypt without health documents, the *quarantina*, which looked like an abandoned elementary school, had its other uses as well, apparently, since my vaccinations and the like were all perfectly in order, no medical tests were given to me, and I was finally reunited with my stuff—except for a couple of tapes and pages of notes from my little steno pad.

An English-speaking Libyan more or less befriended me, probably as much out of curiosity as amicability. His father, I remember, was a backer of what he called "political organizations" out of favor with the Egyptian authorities and the owner of a couple of soap factories someplace. He told me it happened to him every time he came to Cairo. It had nothing to do with vaccinations, he said.

Usually his detentions were just for a few hours, but he was on his second day when I met him, and he was getting pretty irritable. For a soap-maker's son, he was a well-traveled chap: he had spent time in the United States and had gone to college in Trenton, I think, for a year. He had relatives in business in New York, he told me, and he loved going to Rome. We were both fans of Chinese Restaurant, the atmospheric rice shop in the suburbs of Khartoum. He made himself my translator and fixer. He warned me about the guards, told me about the low-level Muslim Brotherhood people there, and explained to me that the man in charge of the prison at night would probably ask me for favors. Thanks to him, I got a couple of bottles of water and a little food. Also thanks to him, the only favor the night warden asked of me was to help him get a job in America.

But the mystery man, for me, was the guy in jeans, plaid shirt and a windbreaker with what appeared to be a golfing logo on it. He was Asian and maybe thirty. He wore new white running shoes, which he had managed to keep spotless despite the dust. He looked extremely familiar, but when I tried saying hello, he only smiled and nodded. My Libyan pal didn't know anything about him, except that he didn't speak Arabic, either. But everything about the guy seemed American, from the baseball cap on the top of his head to the toes of his Nike knock-offs—a dressed-down guy in a sea of men in housecoats.

I was standing near him watching some men who were squatting in the dust, obsessively playing a game that involved small rocks. Suddenly, my Libyan guide sidled up next to me and grabbed my arm.

"He's from North Korea," he said.

Knock me *down*. How could somebody look so much like somebody on our side, smile, nod and be generally pleasant, yet come from one of the planet's most repellent nations?

But it could have been worse. He could have been from France.

1.

To an American, everything about France seems as superficially familiar as that North Korean in the quarantine center did to me.

For residents, whether American or French, there are few surprises to daily life: a leisurely lunch at home or at McDo, as McDonald's is called; groceries from Champion; cash from the ATM. The most obvious and remarkable feature of French life is the national affection for endless TV talk shows.

Visitors, on the other hand, see France in perfect, warm light—the result of a few days with a Peter Mayle book or the dim memory of a Truffaut film or a junior year abroad. Recently on NPR, for example, commentator Susan Stamberg explained how the civilized natives of faraway France spend most of their daylight hours eating lunch, and the rest of the day recovering from the experience: "A summer picnic cloth is dotted with bottles of local wine and fine-smelling wedges of cheese and fresh fruit. By the end of lunch, which could last for hours in Gorde, say, or Aix-en-Provence, the bottles are empty and the spirits are full as the picnickers plan tomorrow's menu." I've never had a lunch like that in France. I asked a friend if that sounded even remotely familiar. He said sure—if you're an unemployed alcoholic. Not even bureaucrats can live like Stamberg's Frenchmen. While it's true that many, many French lunch-eaters work for the government, there is honor even among civil servants in France: the vast majority of them spend their afternoons in cranky, permit-denying sobriety.

Stamberg deplored the exportation of the American work ethic to what she called a "European leisure society," one that she thought "we could do well to import, if we could only afford it."

Unfortunately, Europeans can't afford it, either. Most experts, slow-moving French economists included, say France is mired in an economy dragged into stagnation by low productivity, cornered by massive debt and burdened with expensive, failed social programs and policies churned out for decades—centuries, actually—by a micromanaging, centralized, elitist government in Paris. The growth industry in France is not leisure lunches. The fastest growth sectors in France are in ghetto despair, demographic disaster and blind hatred—hard stuff to use to cushion a veiled attack on American values.

In fact, the myth of our "oldest ally" combined with the idea of France as the source of all that is civilized, tasty, drinkable and topless has created a well-mannered fiction so deeply engrained in our view of the world that to disturb it is to cause intellectual distress. French civility has always been a gratifying conceit: We see in France a perfect mixture of stinky cheese, good wine, general anxiety and amusing pomposity. In the fragrant atmosphere of the imagination, all French women are cute, all French men are suave and all the streets are paved with cobbles.

But in fact, France is a rogue nation in the heart of Europe, and therefore one perhaps even more dangerous to the world than North Korea because we in the United States fail to take its animosity and recklessness seriously. We basically *like* the French. So we don't question French motives the way we do North Korean motives. Maybe it's because North Korea lacks a coherent ennobling mythology: nobody from NPR spends the summer in Pyongyang and comes home to gush about the sauces and the folksy, philo-sophical plumbers, or even the salad bars.

Want to compare your Global Rogues?

	France	North Korea
Size	Colorado + Kansas	Smaller than Mississippi
Population	60,000,000 or so	21,600,000
Anti-Semitism	High	Low
Economic health	Awful	Awful
Threat to others	High	High
Ruled by a bureaucratic elite	Yes	Yes
Friendly to China	Yes	Yes
Friendly to U.S.	No	No
Possesses nukes	Yes	Yes
Sells arms to enemies of U.S.	Yes	Yes
Hostilities with U.S.	Began in 1945	Began in 1945
Funny-looking leader	Yes	Yes
Communist control of unions	Yes	Yes
Fertility rate	Negative	Positive
Dogs in restaurants	Under tables	On menu
Loves Michael Moore *and* Jerry Lewis	Oui!	No

So it's close; but on balance, France is slightly worse than North Korea, something the French prove to us time and again. No other country is more reliable in its dealings with the United States than France. They don't like us all the time.

For the most part, collaborators with France come from the left side of the American political spectrum. Yet even the most lib-eral of all U.S. secretaries of state, Madeline Albright—the pecu-liar woman whose feminized formulations (the Israelis, she once said, "need a time-out") were hallmarks of American foreign pol-icy for nearly a decade—knew a rogue state when she saw one. In the spring of 1994, Albright, the Clinton administration's ambas-sador to the UN at the time, gave a speech in which she described a rogue state as one that did not participate easily in the interna-tional community and often tried to sabotage it. Sounds *très français* to me. As Anthony Lake, Bill Clinton's national security advisor from 1993 until 1996, wrote about the other rogue nation, "North Korea's underlying problem is weakness. However successful North Korean president Kim Jong Il is, President Bush should not worry. We are not going to prop up and save . . . North Korea. It is doomed. It doesn't work." Substitute "France" for "North Korea" and "Chirac" for "Kim Jong Il," and Lake's statement gains even more truth.

Because of their goofy behavior before, during and after the conflict in Iraq, behavior that ultimately cost American lives and money, degraded international institutions and made Iraq a Texas-sized piñata, Walter Wells is correct: bashing the French is now suddenly a subgenre of porch-dog journalism (see this book, for example) and ridiculing the Frenchies is currently a pleasing and honorable pastime for many otherwise affable, everyday Americans named Joe who drink six-packs. And vote. The British also despise the French, but at least they've have had the pleasure of shooting at them in wars for the last five hundred years or so. I understand completely that by calling France a rogue state, I may seem to be piling on. But I don't mean it metaphorically. I mean it literally. In every way imaginable, France is the paradigm outlaw nation.

■ ■ ■ ■ ■

ONE OF THE MORE INTERESTING byproducts of George W. Bush's poorly argued foreign policy is the politicization of global relations along American partisan lines. Chirac, after all, is a right-center guy. Jean-Marie Le Pen's extreme right National Front dislikes us even more than Chirac does. The Socialists think we're all fascists. The French, right and left, don't know much about American political arts, but they know what they don't like. It's George W. Bush. He's their Pimpernel, and they really loathe him. If I had a dollar for every time in the last year some French citizen told me that he didn't actually hate America—"it's Boosh"—I'd have $43.50 (one guy said "your right-wing fanatics"). I know they don't really mean it. They hated America when Bill Clinton was president, too, criticizing American policy objectives in the Middle East, in the Balkans and elsewhere just as much then as now. You couldn't even bomb a Sudanese aspirin factory without howls of outrage wafting above Paris, eating holes in the ozone of common sense. In fact, as the *International Herald Tribune*'s John Vinocur has pointed out, it was for Clinton's America that France's *hyperodieux* former foreign minister, Hubert Védrine, invented the word *hyperpuissance,* now a fashionable anti-American pejorative. The French would hate America if Jacques Cousteau were president, even though he's both French and dead.

The extent of French disgust with us can be measured a zillion ways, but one of my favorite is to see what's in the French papers every September 11. Typically, they all devote their passionate attention to the anniversary of another 9/11 event: the overthrow of the Chilean government of Salvadore Allende in a military coup backed by the CIA. In 2003 it was the subject of a whole series of pieces in *Le Monde* leading up to the anniversary of the day itself. (Other leftist newspapers had the same idea: in the *Guardian,* the consciousness-raiser was an emotional "special report" devoted to "the other September 11." *Le Monde*'s version: "Chile, 1973: The Other September 11.")

The commemorative pieces aren't really necessary. After all, everyone in France already knows what hideous evil was wrought by the Great Satan thirty years ago in Santiago when the United States gave its support to the Chilean military. You can argue your Chateau Thierry and your Belleau Wood and your Normandy beaches and your Marshall Plan all you want. On the great moral tally sheet of the left, all that stuff is easily trumped by American complicity in the overthrow of Allende, a ruthless Marxist ideologue transformed by an adoring press into a secular saint.

America's September 11? Just another day in the downward spiral of American prestige in the French press, where finer minds appreciate nuance and complexity far beyond the ken of your average Texas Republican. In 2001, *Le Monde* famously libeled U.S. citizens everywhere by proclaiming, "We Are All Americans." (Perhaps it should have been "We Are All Chileans.") It took about a year and a half for *Le Monde,* in May 2003, to print a retraction in the form of an editorial beneath a headline admitting, "We Are Non-Americans." What's *that?* In a September 11, 2003, Mondo piece called "Two Years Afterward," George W. Bush is seen as ridiculous for being "convinced that the civilized world is engaged in a new world war against a new totalitarianism" and for not paying attention to America's *"alliés traditionnels,"* a term that *Le Monde* uses without apparent irony, despite the fact that they mean France.

The French right has an obvious problem with September 11, because to express solidarity with America is a historical impossibility. The French left has an equally obvious problem with September 11, because to express solidarity with America is an ideological impossibility. "Support" was for lunchtime on September 12, 2001. By dinner, the prevailing sentiment was disdain. In Italy each 9/11, many newspapers may still run front-page letters from the president of Italy to the president of the United States expressing solidarity in the fight against terrorism. And even in wretched Germany in 2004, most newspapers, including the leftist *Suddeutsche Zeitung,* passed on the chance to wax sardonic and made do with fairly straightforward accounts of the commemorations in the United States and elsewhere. In France, most papers ran with the kind of stories far more comforting to those drunk on anti-Americanism.

In fact, for a nation like France, where make-believe victories are given to he who clings most tightly to the moral edge, the Allende coup is just one more reason for French gratitude, since it supports their caricature of American imperialism while disguising their own failures. This maneuver was evident in the weeks before the Iraq invasion. First, there was the Security Council controversy, which couldn't have come at a better time for Chirac.

The U.S.'s plea for UN support provided a lofty hedge behind which his government was able to hide its dismal economic performance while Chirac tried in vain to build support for some lame but desperately needed pension reforms.

Then came America's bizarre, grotesque returns to the UN looking for support. These were mystifying, for it was France's refusal to negotiate resolutions concerning Iraq that effectively destroyed the UN's admittedly limited usefulness to begin with. When President Bush sent Colin Powell back to the Security Council the first time, in August 2003, for some postwar assistance, it was Chirac and Villepin who got the benefit of a pleasant distraction from their real problems. Having mastered the rhetoric of pomposity by denouncing America's "logic of war" before the Iraq invasion, Villepin simply expressed his sorrow at America's "logic of occupation" while advancing France's love for the "logic of sovereignty," so long as it's France's sovereignty. It turns out that only a month before, Villepin personally commandeered a French air force plane, loaded it with a few medics, a security unit from the French foreign intelligence service (DGSE) and one of his own senior aides, and had the thing flown to the Brazilian-Colombian border—without actually bothering to ask Brazilian authorities for permission to do so. Monsieur Multipolarité's plan? To pick up an old family friend, Ingrid Betancourt, who had been abducted by Colombian FARC guerrillas, as part of a deal that would have provided French medical care to an ailing Colombian terrorist leader. When the Brazilians expressed outrage and demanded to board the aircraft, Villepin's man claimed diplomatic immunity for the plane and its contents. When the story broke, Villepin quickly arranged his cover with French president Jacques Chirac and then defaulted to French form: retreat and apology.

The "logic of sovereignty" may be more repugnant, in the end, than France's law of indifference. The rest of France, by and large, ignores Paris, where the business of manufacturing French *gloire* and its wretched byproduct, *les exceptions,* goes on unhindered by the facts of history. Outside that awful precinct, the French pay little attention to their government, ignore the national newspapers and, for the most part, simply shrug off those laws and edicts they consider to be violations of nature. Most of them are busy trying to work around the obstructions thrown up by a central government obsessed with ruling by statute, regulation and decree, as if it would be possible to govern France well if only the correct combination of numbers were dialed in.

Unfortunately, Friedrich Hayek's famous Road to Serfdom still runs right through the middle of the country: The state not only manipulates the economy in its traditional, heavy-handed way, it also manipulates the measures of success—"credentials" are everything in elite-infested France—and of human freedom, including the freedom to use hard work as a means of getting ahead.

The result is a nation reliant on a kind of pervasive bribery, one that promises citizens a basket of expensive "rights"—including paid vacations, free health care, free university tuition, a huge educational bureaucracy that acts as day care for French kids as young as two, pensions that are literally larger than life and work-weeks that, by law, stop at thirty-five hours no matter what. Hovering over all these guarantees are mammoth national unions, like the CGT, the last redoubt of France's once-mighty Communist Party. Intransigent, narrow, ruthless, the unions regard reforms as anathema. Yet even though reforms are desperately needed, huge subsidies nevertheless dominate every sector of the economy, while bloated, intrusive bureaucracies oversee every aspect of life. All these things are seen as part of the cost of life in modern France. If you want to see a perfectly performed Gallic shrug, simply ask about the cost of any of them.

2.

SERFDOM. IT'S A EUROPEAN WAY of life—and nowhere is this more true than in France, where ruling elites occupy seats of power heavily upholstered with a soft cushion of fat, expensive bureaucracy supported by enormous tax burdens on the workers. In France, the state is by far the largest employer. When voter apathy threatens to change to irritation, tens of thousands of new government bureaucrats are employed, all of them eager supporters of yet more government. When France made it illegal for most people to work more than thirty-five hours a week, those with an entrepreneurial spirit may have suffered; but government workers sure didn't complain. The national government may be expensive, distant and dull, but at least it isn't annoying the voters with concerns about sacrifices, or even about responsibility. In France, the workers work, the rulers rule—and neither does a very good job. At dinner with a French civil servant recently, we talked about the famous headscarf ban imposed amidst much fanfare by posturing French politicians as a way of articulating the country's dedication to *laïcité*, the mythic ideal of secularism that's supposed to make clear the role of the Church in France, but doesn't. Muslims hated the ban; Christians didn't care. The burden of the law fell on local school administrators. I asked one about how the headscarf ban would be enforced locally. "By a man on the phone in Paris," was his sardonic reply, meaning the central government would apply the pressure, while the local officials were left to apply the law.

The French may pride themselves on the separation of church and state, but the real separation in the French Republic has been between those who rule and those who are ruled. This certainly wasn't the apparent intention of the revolutionaries of 1789. One of their first pieces of work was the creation of a "Declaration of the Rights of Man"—a typically inflated title for an equivocating, vacillating version of the American Declaration of Independence.

Consisting of a preamble that in places reads more like Bentham than Jefferson ("... in order that the grievances of the citizens, based hereafter upon simple and incontestable principles, shall tend to the maintenance of the constitution and redound to the happiness of all ...") and seventeen articles, the document contains more loopholes than a shag carpet. Consider, for example, the very first article: "Men are born and remain free and equal in rights. Social distinctions may be founded only upon the general good."

In other words, men may be free and all that, but some social distinctions separating them are cool, so long as whoever's in charge says it's necessary for the "general good." Hence, one of De Gaulle's first projects after liberation was the establishment of the École nationale d'administration—French for "Social Distinction U"—where the country's governing elite would be trained to keep the electorate in its comfortable place. Like *Le Monde* but more closely controlled, it was one of De Gaulle's postwar inventions, created to give tangibility to the chauvinism that his myth of *La France* required.

Understanding the role of the ENA is perhaps the easiest way to make sense of a political culture that is so closed, so elitist that it highlights the hypocrisy of France's droning appeal for the moral high ground. ENA graduates—called *énarques*—run everything in France. ENA types rise instantly to the top: they do not handle middle-management positions well. Everybody who milks the big government *vache* in France is an *énarque*—Chirac, Juppé, Jospin, Balladur, Fabius, Giscard. Six of the last eight prime ministers have been *énarques*. If your father was an *énarque*, chances are you will be one, too.

Theoretically a product of meritocracy, the École nationale d'administration is the ultimate insider's network, obliterating the normal ideological boundaries that inform modern politics. The current center-right cabinet is packed with *énarques;* the cabinet in the previous Socialist government was, too. Right or left, if you're from the ENA, you rule. It would be easier for a conservative Republican to be elected senator from Massachusetts than it would be for a non-ENA grad to be appointed to run, say, France's finances. All together, there are some 4,500 *énarques* at work in France; three-quarters of them occupy the most powerful slots in the government bureaucracy; the rest, according to Jon Henly, writing in Britain's *Guardian* newspaper, run public-sector and other companies in which the government is an important stakeholder. The ubiquity of *énarques* in positions of power is simply a given, one of many that have contrived to invest the true Gallic shrug with such authenticity that only a native can do it with conviction. Men like Juppé and Chirac may be corrupt, but the alternative would be real reform, and *nobody* in charge of reform wants that.

Certainly nobody with an *énarque* pedigree wants it. In fact, the elites exist to perpetuate elitism, not to guide the French nation to progress, since, by liberal definition, that would require elevating as many humans as possible to elite status. Instead, supply is limited, much the same way De Beers limits the number of diamonds that reach the market. Every year, the ENA mines schools for the best students in the country and offers around 150 of them the chance to enjoy some serious social distinctions. (The best of the rest go to one of the other, marginally less powerful *grandes écoles*, Sciences Po and the École polytechnique.) The entrance exam is tough, to say the least: it takes three days and culminates in *le grand oral*—an interview that lasts just under an hour and is the equivalent of an experiment in amateur dentistry. After a little more than two years, the twenty most successful students are given plum jobs pulling one of the levers on the machinery of government. The rest are made to wait a little longer, but they too eventually float to the surface, most going into the bureaucracy, some into the private sector.

As a class, they function like a benign Comintern—a group of insiders who have enormous power, very little of which is used for the good of the state or its people, but most of which is used to cement their "social distinction." Politically and culturally, they are a cancer of corruption. And they feed and protect their own. For example, the French government backed out of an agreement to pay fines in the prosecution of a fraud case associated with Executive Life, the California company purchased, apparently illegally, by Crédit lyonnais. The sticking point? U.S. prosecutors wanted to be able to target individual French businessmen implicated in the apparent swindle, including François Pinault, who is an École nationale d'administration graduate, a businessman and media mogul, one of the richest men in France—and, naturally, a close friend of Jacques Chirac's.

Paradoxically, the enshrinement of ENA graduates as a privileged class does not mean that others are excluded from sharing in the spoils of government, provided they have what it takes to muscle their way to the trough. As a rule, what it takes is a lot of money and the clout of a big business behind you to back it up. While the *énarques* have more poster boys than 'N Sync, ironically one of those who best exemplifies France's ruling class is seventy-seven-year-old Charles Pasqua, a working-class stiff who has made good by playing politics with the instinctive skill of a natural-born grifter.

A former Corsican beach bum who got his start selling *pastis* and cigarettes, Pasqua made his way to the top tier of boozedom, becoming Ricard's international operations director in 1962. Four years later, when he met Jacques Chirac, he moved into the upper echelons of French political society with the finesse of a homeless in-law and quickly became Jacques's bag man.

Pasqua is a poorly educated thug, a source of constant embarrassment to the *énarques* with whom he rubs shoulders. He dresses like a bad character actor in a collection of ill-fitting suits, and he speaks French with a thick Corsican accent. He's the kind of man from whom you'd gladly buy a used car, because you know he'd kill you if you didn't. He's a living Hoffa, a godless godfather,

J. Edgar Hoover without the dresses. He is vociferously anti-
American, and perhaps because of that and his image as the perfect anti-*énarque,* when he arrived on the scene he promptly became
a populist hero, playing to the same crowd of neofascist cranks
that supported Le Pen. Chic Parisians, fond of his immigrant- and
Yank-bashing rhetoric, sent him to the legislature first in 1967. By
1986, when Chirac became prime minister, Pasqua had become
such a fixture of the inner circle that he was made interior minister. Pasqua became France's top cop.

This secured his position as one of the most influential politicians in France, and he quickly made his office into an instrument
for inflicting trauma on those with whom he disagreed. Overnight,
the Interior Ministry became very much a for-profit enterprise.

In 1988, when French hostages were taken in Lebanon, the
French government allegedly paid a ransom of millions. The deal
was handled by one of Pasqua's loyal underlings, Jean-Charles
Marchiani, who, according to a leaked government memo, siphoned
off a steep "commission" into a Swiss bank account.

In 1994, Marchiani and Pasqua brokered a deal to sell Exo-
cet missiles to Iran in violation of international agreements,
allegedly pocketing kickbacks in the deal. According to newspaper accounts, the weapons were shipped from an Algerian military base on a civilian aircraft to France, from there to Cyprus and
from Cyprus to Iran.

The next year, Pasqua really got down to business.

■ He played kingmaker in the presidential contest between
Chirac, Lionel Jospin and Edouard Balladur: first, organizing an
illegal fundraising scheme for Balladur; then, when Balladur fal-
tered in the polls and fingered Pasqua as the bad guy, making a
deal with Chirac that swung the election in his favor.

■ While manipulating the presidential race, Pasqua was also
busy forcing a French journalist to seek asylum in the United States
after the writer linked Pasqua and Ricard to drug operations in
Morroco. U.S. authorities rushed approval for the request once it

was clear to them that the man would be in danger if left to the mercy of French police.

■ That same year, without consulting the Foreign Ministry, Pasqua launched the "William Lee Affair," part of a unilateral move to throw alleged CIA agents out of Paris, none of whom was named "William Lee." Lee, in reality, was a lawyer who had the misfortune of crossing paths with some of France's big-business and political elites.

What was William Lee's sin? "The answer . . . ," wrote David Ignatius in the *Washington Post*, "appears to lie in a lawsuit Lee filed in 1993, challenging the merger of two big French companies—the arms maker Matra and the publishing giant Hachette. The suit argued that the December 1992 merger had cheated Matra shareholders because it had not taken into account a secret contract worth roughly $1.5 billion, signed the previous month, to sell Matra missiles to Taiwan."

Lee protested his innocence, and the U.S. government backed him up. His sole interest, he claimed, was to win a case and make some money.

"But to jittery government and business leaders in Paris," wrote Ignatius, "the challenge to a big French defense company appeared to be part of a broad CIA plot to undermine France's corporate interests. The French believed the CIA had helped torpedo contracts for French firms in Saudi Arabia and Brazil, and they saw the assault on Matra as another example of CIA meddling."

According to Ignatius' report, "[Lee] was summoned . . . to the U.S. Embassy in Paris. The embassy security officer warned him that his life was in danger and advised him to leave France immediately. When he arrived in Washington the following week, a deputy assistant secretary of state named Mark Mulvey told him to take the death threats seriously."

Uri Dan and Dennis Eisenberg of the *Jerusalem Post*, however, saw even more the diplomatic dustup:

For the last year and a half, [France's] most skilled commercial diplomats and businessmen have been trying to negotiate massive deals with Iraqi President Saddam Hussein and the Iranian mullahs under a great cloak of secrecy.

These countries are traditional French markets. The French were the major suppliers to Baghdad, enabling Saddam to build a nuclear-bomb manufacturing facility. This posed such a danger to Israel that then Prime Minister Menachem Begin ordered its destruction from the air in 1981. It was also the French who nurtured and encouraged Ayatollah Ruhollah Khomeini to return to Tehran to topple the shah. Why? To rid Iran of American influence and win lucrative deals. Jobs would be created in France, and industrial magnates would rake in vast profits. . . .

Both Iraq and Iran still owe the French hundreds of millions of dollars. The only way Paris can hope to get its money back is to give Iraq and Iran what they want. At the top of their shopping list is the machinery and know-how to build weapons of mass destruction, both conventional and unconventional. . . .

It is no secret in Western and CIA circles that the French intelligence service has been frantically trying to hide its government's Machiavellian wheeling and dealing with Iraq and Iran. Nor is it a secret that the CIA does not need its Paris staff to reveal French dealing. They get all the information they want, and more besides, from their extensive electronic surveillance system, as well as from friendly allies.

So what lies behind the French government's sudden decision to pretend that it is hot under the collar about CIA men working in Paris, particularly since Pasqua fully understands the danger of Islamic fundamentalism? The answer is simple: politics.

In France, when Pasqua pitches, politics is not *le softball.*

By the end of the 1990s, four different investigations were devoted to Pasqua's scams, including one for money-laundering and another for Pasqua's specialty, the weapons deal, this one involving Angola, Mitterrand's son, and Marchiani.

That's one more than the three investigations that were closing the noose on Chirac when he took office as president and immediately passed a law that made it impossible to charge sitting officials, including legislators, with corruption or any other crime except "high treason," which in France is even worse than speaking English. The law was passed as part of the legislative package that included France's agreement to become part of the International Criminal Court in The Hague because the French invented irony. By 2003, Pasqua had moved into the big time, even in the context of French government corruption.

In 1996, the sanctions that had been in place against Iraq since the first Gulf War were modified to allow money from the sale of Iraqi oil to be used to provide Iraqi citizens with food and medicine. The program was administered by the United Nations, who turned it over to Saddam Hussein, who was given the authority to award vouchers for oil to those who helped the regime. According to a U.S. government report released in October 2004 by chief U.S. weapons inspector Charles Duelfer, officials in France, Russia and China were given vouchers that could be redeemed for cash, based on the prevailing price of oil. High on the list of those named by the report was Charles Pasqua. According to a former Chirac aide, speaking to FOX News's Bill O'Reilly, Pasqua, along with other associates and business interests close to Chirac, harvested more than 75 million barrels of oil, stealing money that was supposed to have gone to the Iraqi poor. The Duelfer report also noted that Saddam had promised France access to Iraq's undeveloped oil assets as well.

After being routinely re-elected for decades, Pasqua was finally tossed out by the voters. In 2004, he lost a bid for re-election as a member of the European Parliament. Faced with joining his old friend Marchiani in prison, Pasqua called in all his chits. Just weeks ahead of a senatorial election, and with a prosecutor hot on the trail, Chirac worked together with the popular finance minister Nicholas Sarkozy to get Pasqua a seat in the French Senate. In France, Senate seats are awarded by "electoral colleges" made up of local politicians. Those apparatchiks in "Sarkoland"—the Hauts-de-Seine turf of Sarkozy—dutifully sheltered Pasqua. His five-year term expires in 2009, when, if he is still alive, he will be dutifully re-elected, perhaps joining his ally Chirac, if he's unsuccessful holding off Sarko's ambitions, as they both seek sanctuary in the great church of state, where the pews are already filled with corrupt Socialists and their ilk.

■ ■ ■ ■ ■

MOST OF THESE STORIES are only partially reported in the French press, if at all. (The *International Herald Tribune* mirrored the French press's treatment of the Duelfer revelations, for example, covering the protests of the French government at having been named, but ignoring almost completely the charges against Pasqua and others.

The French, however, realize how completely corrupt their government is. Every now and then, the National Assembly makes a muffled anti-*énarque* wheeze, causing the French press to take a look around, discover the insidious presence of *énarques* and their allied elites everywhere, and run a story about the phenomenon. Recently, for example, the editors of the newsweekly *Le Nouvel Observateur* were shocked—*shocked!*—to discover that a "caste" rules France, that it is largely unaccountable to anyone, that it spends lots of money, that it does relatively little, and that it is in no danger of disappearing so long as the French remain dependent on the state for the existence of any economy at all. The report wasn't exactly a masterpiece of investigative journalism; most of the stuff came from *Les Intouchables,* Ghislaine Ottenheimer's latest book on the *énarques.* The not-very-surprising verdict: the people running France are hopelessly corrupt, an "absolute brake on innovation," in the words of one political critic. As one occasionally troublemaking parliamentarian, Alain Madelin, put it, *"L'Irlande a l'IRA. L'Espagne a l'ETA. L'Italie a la mafia. La France a l'ÉNA."* ("Britain has the IRA, Spain has ETA, Italy has the Mafia and France has the ENA.")

These Antoinettes ride through life on the backs of the common folk, the hardworking *fraternité* who cannot aspire to grow up and become self-published poets, like Villepin. Optimism is an insanity, and after a while, the burden gets to be too much to ignore. "This whole place is falling apart," a normally sedate businessman, the director of one of the biggest companies in his sector, told me in the spring of 2004 over a dinner in Paris. "There's nothing left, no money, no hope, nothing."

At $140 for two little pieces of undercooked fish, he wasn't kidding. And his despair was no joke, either. Doubt, fear and pessimism are at the heart of what it is to be French in the twenty-first century.

3.

In the part of rural Pennsylvania where we seem to have accidentally aggregated real estate and to which we default when we aren't living in France, going to town means traveling for more than an hour, dodging quick deer and slow Amish, only to end up in Altoona. "What town are you near?" people ask, and when I say "Altoona" they look at an empty space somewhere over my shoulder. The truth is, in that part of Pennsylvania you're not very close to anything except Protestants.

From the road you can see their huge metal buildings, their recreation centers, their vast parking lots and playgrounds, worshipers dressed as for golf, and the signs that proclaim "Jesus Is Lord" and "Sin Kills, Jesus Saves." Spirituality exists to the extent it does in America because of Protestant vigor and faith. I love Protestant hymns, and when I pass a crowded church, I always start humming "How Great Thou Art," then realize I can't get the melody out of my mind without breaking into a quick verse of "It's a Small World, After All," and you know where that leads.

My family's parish church, on the other hand, isn't Protestant. It's Eastern Orthodox. It's almost as far from us as Altoona

94

is, but in a different direction, next to a river in a quiet little hamlet where there used to be a quarry, which is now closed. The church is quite lovely, but you could put the whole thing in a corner of one of those Protestant recreation buildings and still have room to shoot hoops for Jesus.

The dozen or so parishioners know each other like family, because, for the most part, they are—the children of men and women who came to the United States from Eastern Europe in the early years of the twentieth century. But they are also very old now, and every so often the patient priest who has been their pastor for more than a quarter-century grimly buries one of them and comes back the next Sunday to preach a homily to a smaller congregation. Because we spend many months at a time outside the country, I can see the parish shrink with every visit. These days, when I arrive with my pretty wife and my three cheerful, young daughters, I feel like a zany florist making an emergency call. But a parish is about numbers, so I dread the day when we show up, try the door, find it locked, turn around and drive home quietly.

I was telling a man in New York City about this church and its aging, shrinking congregation surrounded by all that bustling nondenominational Protestant success. "Well," he said, "the solution is obvious. You people are so *exclusive* with that communion business of yours. You have to get other people in there. Be *diverse.* Then maybe people would come and have a good time and you could save that little church." I pointed out that this would actually make it into something very different, something very non-Orthodox—in fact, something rather, shall we say, *Protestant,* when there were already plenty of those to go around. But he only shrugged. "Gotta do whatcha gotta do," he said.

That's a French solution if I ever heard one. It reflects exactly the problem that everyone in France acknowledges but never really discusses: In order to save France, they have to make it into something very different, something distinctly non-French, something actually quite, oh, Islamic. You can count the reasons, because they're all right there in the numbers. The aging demographic of the country is making it harder and harder to be a believer in the extensive system of benefits and programs that constitute a modern European state. When this awkward truth is discussed, it all comes out wrong. Recently, for example, a writer for the *International Herald Tribune* tried to spread some cheer in the heart o' darkness by headlining a story, "Europe's Economic Woes: Oversold?" The buoyant paragraph:

> The demographic horror story—in which the structure crumbles because there are too few workers being forced to pay taxes to support too many retirees—may be oversold. There is an ample supply of extra workers available via immigration, and while there is great reluctance to let them in, and more than a little discrimination against hiring those that are already in Europe, that can be seen as an untapped resource.

So simple! In France, the solution to how to repair a broken social security system is simply to replace French people with *other* people! Ingenious, really—and as long as France took its brutal mission of "civilizing" the world seriously, this might have worked. But France has given that up and now looks to the impoverished people of the undeveloped world as "an untapped resource" to exploit in order to avoid pension reform. That way, sometime in the next twenty years or so, a couple of imported "Frenchmen"— probably the bitter, *banlieu*-squatting Muslim sons of an angry Moroccan immigrant—will be working happily to support a European Frenchman who will exist on a pension and demand more money every year.

But there are two problems here. First, France has already surrendered in its effort to help the less developed nations of the world, except to take their oil and manipulate their foreign policy. If the "untapped resource" of poor people from the Third World is to be maintained, it just won't do to make them *less* poor. The other problem: the French Muslims of the future may not be inclined to support the Frenchman of today in the manner to which he has become accustomed.

The Cato Institute's José Pinera explained the bad news in a recent issue of the *Cato Journal*:

> The population of Europe is aging and declining. A trend that could have been perfectly manageable with foresight could turn into a catastrophe given the increasing unfunded liabilities arising from pay-as-you-go (PAYGO) public pension programs, now more than 200 percent of GDP in France and Italy, and more than 150 percent of GDP in Germany. This situation is especially difficult in a continent where entitlements are deeply entrenched in a welfare state culture.

Those happy projections haven't quite sunk into the unionized noggins of those French people who euphemistically call themselves "workers." The pensions debate has now grown stale in France, mired every year in sullen, angry strikes at the slightest hint of reform, and escalating demands that can't be met in the real world. Dominique de Villepin, the sensitive former foreign minister of France and permanent cat's paw for Chirac, is now in charge of the Interior Ministry, following in the footsteps of one of the few competent French politicians in government today, Nicholas Sarkozy. Chirac is a very old, corrupt man who needs a lackey in the mold of Pasqua to be in charge of the police who, he fears, may one day arrest him. Sarkozy, Chirac's eager, ambitious political rival and the most popular politician in France, is young and relatively unsullied. Their conflict is not ideological; they are from the same party. The conflict is over real estate: Sarkozy wants Chirac's safe house in the Elysée. Hence the hatred between them.

If Sarkozy is successful, Chirac will go to jail, unless he can find refuge in the Senate. No wonder Chirac sent Sarko off to political hell in the Finance Ministry, where he was charged with trying to implement reforms to stave off France's inevitable financial despair. He had lots of enemies. The CGT, the national trade union and France's last bastion of Communist influence, didn't try to inspire an environment of compromise: even stage technicians went on strike at the first hint of reform. That, by the way, meant a "cultural crisis," as some in the French press called it. Just think. No (state-subsidized, underattended, overperformed) Molière!

Meanwhile, Villepin's public pronouncements were flamboyant and meaningless enough to make up for any absent theatrical events, even if they were mostly designed to help him outmaneuver Sarkozy and prevent the younger man from ousting Chirac. For example, the part-time poet wasted several thousand words before he told *Le Monde* that with him in charge of the Interior Ministry, "everyone can find a place in France." That comment meant little in real-life terms, of course.

For the sake of political expedience, Chirac has not only squandered his country's position in Europe and the West, but also mortgaged its future. His failures will outlast him by a long, long way: France in fifty or a hundred years will not be a happy place—the sad consequence of all that centralized wisdom that is the hallmark of every French government. In the week preceding Bastille Day 2003, when *le président de la république* is always called upon to speak to his lowly *citoyens* by way of a television appearance, more than 70 percent of them wanted Chirac to explain how he proposed to fix the pension problem. In 2004, they still wanted to know. In 2005, they'll want the same thing. It's a question they will go on asking until the Grand Mufti, delivering his annual address from the Elysée, but under the star and *croissant*, finally tells them to move to Algeria if they don't like living in France.

The inescapable fact is that in order to keep their full barge of benefits afloat, France needs many, many more Frenchmen. While the French are geniuses at making more French bureaucrats (thirty-eight thousand new ones last year alone, reported *Le Figaro*), God in His ironic wisdom has made it difficult for the French to make actual Frenchmen. So they do what the *International Herald Tribune* has advised: they import them from Algeria,

Tunisia and Morocco. Meanwhile, North African Muslims apparently have no problem making *many* more Muslims, who become the heirs to the nation.

Something like 2 percent of French Christians attend church on any given Sunday, but almost 100 percent of them practice birth control and "family planning," a euphemism for having a family that includes more cars than kids. About 100 percent of French Muslims go to their local mosque every Friday, but only about 2 percent of them practice birth control. Sometime this century, France will become a Muslim state, at which point France's war with America no doubt will take an interesting turn.

Natural law, the richly ornamented expression of which is conventional religious practice and belief, is easy to disregard. But you break the law, you pay the price. And in the case of France—and Germany and Italy, for that matter—the price of being fruitless and not multiplying is a shrinking state welfare apparatus and a working life that will either have to rely on unlimited immigration or have to stretch out longer and longer until it takes you right up to the edge of the grave, then pushes you in. For those who *need* to believe that the state can always do what God cannot, that's called dying for your faith.

As Chirac makes clear every year in his Bastille Day *intervention*, pensions aren't the only problem he isn't confronting. The headache of Corsican politics, a duplicitous foreign policy, the ongoing appeal of the National Front, an economy the projected growth of which is expressed in teeny fractions, an immigrant problem that knows no boundaries, and a debt that is swelling beyond the legal limits of the European Union are all confounding Chirac's attempt to do what Tony Blair and Bill Clinton did—appear to seize the center by co-opting the opposition's issues. It's easy as pie. But it's never that simple when you try to say it in French.

If the only issue that Chirac had to deal with were his war with America, he'd be the god he thinks he is and all French people would fall down before him. But the complications facing France can't be articulated by simplistic political rhetoric, so Chirac, having bored the voters with his anti-Americanism, is falling in the polls and hoping to talk his way back into favor, while shrinking the voters' expectations.

If he weren't so French, he'd thank God for giving him such an inept, fragmented left-wing opposition. But whoever succeeds Chirac will face the same mess. The shrinking stature of France— diplomatic, economic, intellectual, spiritual, political, military— is a remarkable thing. One day, I'm sure, I'll go to bash the French and find myself making faces instead at the Greater Belgium hidden behind the great curtain of twentieth-century pretence and folly.

What to do? *Rien*. In France, the average Jo assumes the worst from his leaders, anyway. When Chirac rolled out one of his semi-annual economic reform speeches, *Le Nouvel Observateur* compared him to Emile Coué, the pioneering champion of a typical French contribution to modern culture—autosuggestion. Coué told his patients to repeat the phrase "Every day, and in every way, I am becoming better and better" over and over until they thought it was true.

Not even the French are that dumb. Besides, they have better ways to become better, *merci*. They know their government stifles initiative and enterprise and Hoovers their wallets to do it. So most French citizens simply collude in the corruption forced on them. Not just small jobs and minor repairs are conducted under the table, hidden from the taxman's spiraling eye; entire communities are built "on the black" in untraceable and therefore untaxable transactions, with everybody from the surveyor to the carpet layer paid in cash. Many Americans may not have much regard for the French government, but the disdain that the French themselves have for France's government is astonishing. The entire country is in revolt. But this is France, so they aren't taking up arms against an oppressive government. They are simply ignoring it.

4.

The problem of Islamification, however, can't be as easily ignored. Nobody really knows how many Muslims there are in France— say 15 percent or ten million and you wouldn't be too far off. France contains Europe's greatest concentration of Islamic immigrants, legal and otherwise. In a conventional state, immigration is not the emotional issue it is in France, one of the most screwed-up developed nations on earth. But in France, the assumption is that all French people are alike and are all obedient followers of the law—especially the one that separates church and state. Multiculturalism, the knee-jerk religion of Western sociologists, does not exist in France. There are no African-Frenchmen and no Polish-Frenchmen. Frenchmen come in only one flavor: French Vanilla. If you're a citizen, you're French and nothing more. That's how the French are able to justify giving away their country to Muslims. The French government simply slaps a big "Frenchman" sticker on the back of all those passing burnouses and goes back to sleep.

The trouble is, Algerian and Moroccan "Frenchmen" don't look very French, at least to other Frenchmen, nor do they act very French. So the Muslims from North Africa are integrated geographically and statutorily only. In every other respect, they're outsiders. After comparing the forty thousand houses of worship belonging to France's 45 million Catholics with the relative handful of Islamic mosques, Chris Caldwell, an astute analyst of, among other things, the French for the *Weekly Standard* and other publications, wrote (in the *Atlantic*):

> The unequal position of Islam makes it harder for Muslims to integrate two ways.... First, it radicalizes the religion in practice, because freelance "mosques" tend to be set up by poorly trained, fiery, self-appointed imams. Given the interplay between religion and politics in Islam, this in turn radicalizes Muslims' politics.

Second, the formal mosques that do exist are funded by foreign Islamic governments often hostile to France's interests. Paris's grand mosque is mainly funded by the government of Algeria, others by [Wahhabist] Saudi Arabia. This can lead the *française de souche* to suspect—sometimes with justification—that their Muslim fellow citizens constitute a kind of fifth column. And no justification is needed for their suspicions.

This is reinforced, Caldwell notes, by the "humiliating debacle" of the Algerian war. In the eyes of many Frenchmen, Caldwell adds, a Muslim is "a symbol of French failure."

Mostly, though, the French shrug off this problem and keep it far from the concerns of everyday life. But every now and then, something disturbs the slumber of happy France. One such disturbance came when the government decided that Muslim schoolgirls were not sufficiently French because they were wearing headscarves to school, as required of women by Islamic law. But in France, the law that matters is the law of fashion. Hermès, as you recall, was the infidel messenger of the gods. And what he told the French, apparently, was that they should wear really expensive silk scarves on their heads to display their sensitivity to fashion and to indicate their wealth. So perhaps it isn't surprising that French politicians and journalists truly believed that the most pressing social issue facing France had to do with whether or not girls should be allowed to go to school with their heads covered.

The problem is the statement behind the fashion, and how that statement violates the sense of secular propriety that governs one of the key French myths of their *république*. If a Muslim girl's scarf statement is a reflection of obedience to fashion, there is no problem here, monsieur. But if her taste in headwear is so lousy that the scarf statement suggests proselytism, there is a very large problem.

It's not really that the government fears Islamic schoolgirls will convert the French to a religion that bans drinking and topless sunbathing. It's that nobody in France is allowed to represent

herself as a member of a proscribed group, most of which are religious. After all, there's a uniform in France for most every other
cohort—butchers, bakers, mechanics and bankers. But God for-
bid you should wear a religious symbol. When my daughters first
attended a French public school, they mistakenly wore their little silver Orthodox crosses over their sweaters. They were promptly
instructed to hide them, but not out of fear that the children on
the playground would be seized with a need to return to the Julian
calendar. Rather, it is forbidden to even hint that you are a person
of religious convictions, period. It is acceptable in the secular state
to send a girl to school looking like a hooker, because at least
hookers aren't *nuns*. But there is a great fear in France that if you
send your Muslim daughter to school looking like a character from
a Laura Ingalls Wilder book, so that other children realize they
are in the company of somebody who embraces Allah, it will create a threat to the state. Obviously, this says more about the fragility
of the state than about danger to children.

The problem of Islamic girls wearing scarves to school and
Islamic women wearing scarves to work had been simmering in
France for a long time before it started erupting in the press in
2003. But it's not the head covering that's the problem; it's what's
in the head being covered. Chirac's declaration that "there is something aggressive" about the Muslim veil, and the predictable fem-
inist view as expressed in an open letter published in *Elle* from
prominent Frenchwomen urging a ban on headscarves because
they represent the submission of women, pretty much reflected
the view of the issue from the right and from the left. It was clear
that something had to be done.

What was done was to appoint a government commission to
investigate the headscarf issue and tell the president of the *république*
what should be done about it. When the report was issued by the
unfortunately named Stasi Commission (after Bernard Stasi, the
chairman), the recommendations surprised no one. No headscarves!
said Stasi. This would help prevent sullying the secular purity of

public schools and offices, the government claimed. Not only that, but according to a mysterious Reuters report, the government also claimed that "Muslim practices in schools, combined with opposition to Israeli repression against Palestinians, may fuel anti-Semitism."

So, problem solved. The French media and the governing elite were transfixed by the importance and cleverness of what they read they had done. On French TV and on radio, the story drowned out every other issue normally preoccupying the French media, including the celebrity *du jour.* Even the French press's Yank-bashing thugs took a breather and gave way to the reportage devoted to the way Islamic schoolgirls dress.

The reason for their fascination was obvious—and a perfect example of *légicentrisme,* the French art of attacking a critical, complex social issue by focusing on the most superficial aspect of it, then passing a goofy law that revises common sense and makes it dumb. The real problems associated with the rampant Islamification of the French state won't be solved by issuing a dress decree, because banning headscarves completely misses the point: French Muslims are Muslims in France, not French people who just happen to be Muslim—the way French Christians are French people who *very* incidentally happen to be Christian. The uncounted Muslims in France are many things, including angry, ghettoized, trivialized, and pandered to by an endless stream of elitist politicians. But the one thing they are not is French—at least not French as the French understand it. As a result, crime is rampant; and the public, the media, the politicians, even the authors of the Stasi report itself all know who is responsible. If they still can't figure it out, Islamic fundamentalists abroad are happy to help.

■ ■ ■ ■ ■

THE KIDNAPPING IN AUGUST 2004 of French journalists Georges Malbrunot and Christian Chesnot took the standard playbook of

Iraqi terrorists and wrote a whole new chapter, just for the benefit of the French. The conventional gambit in Iraq is to intimidate governments and businesses into withdrawing from the country by having their soldiers or employees yanked off the street, then beheaded for later broadcast on Al-Jazeerah, every antiwar leftist's favorite network. The result was a wave of appeasement by those on the periphery of the Iraqi conflict—the fifty Philippines soldiers withdrawn from the country is one example. And sometimes the kidnappings and executions are just for drill, such as the murder of twelve Nepalese cooks and cleaners working for a company based in Jordan. They were beheaded or shot because, Ansar al-Sunna announced, they were helping Jews and Christians, even though they were Buddhists.

But the kidnapping of French journalists by yet another band of terrorist cut-throats (or "militants," as Reuters and the *Wall Street Journal* call people who behead other people, including their own employees) seemed a little counterintuitive. It's like a double own-goal: Frenchmen *and* journalists? What were they thinking? Almost every French person in Iraq is there as an apologist for the terrorists—either the ones who are rampaging through the country now or the ones who were in power before the invasion. Besides, France's foreign policy has a long history of mollifying various Arab despots in an effort to keep peace among the Muslims at home. Against a headscarf ban, however, that meant nothing. So the French journalists were kidnapped to force the French government into rescinding the ban. How much leverage did Chirac have against the terrorists? None. He took a meeting with Russia's Vladimir Putin and Germany's Gerhard Schroeder, which *Libération* called a "mobilization." The terrorists didn't take note, so in order to free the journalists, France tried to rely first on the fraternal intervention of Hamas, an anti-Israeli terror group supported by the French, who appealed for the journalists to be set free on the same day that two Hamas suicide bombers attacked buses in Beersheba, killing sixteen innocent passengers and wounding nearly one hundred others, none of whom were French. But not even Hamas's assistance could help. (The two men were released unexpectedly in December 2004. The French denied that a ransom had been paid.)

Sadly for France, and despite its best efforts, sympathy with the devil of terrorism is reflected in the antisocial behavior of many Muslims at home. Those who perpetrate hate crimes against the French are frequently "disaffected" Arabs, mostly from North Africa. They despise America, Jews and, unfortunately for the French, France. More than anyone else, they are responsible for the rapid escalation of French crime in general and anti-Semitism in particular, and there aren't many Frenchmen who would deny it. Hence, the chauvinistic Jean-Marie Le Pen's popularity continues to soar. As of last year, 22 percent of French voters supported him, which means he would still give the Socialists and the other leftist parties hell in an election. Nicholas Sarkozy, perhaps the only French politician willing to call a Muslim a Muslim, had been diligent in keeping social unrest under control when he had the Interior Ministry; but since 2004, that ministry has been the province of Villepin, and it's an uphill struggle. While large, loud and for the most part empty pronouncements are made about shunting wicked, violence-inspiring Islamic clerics out of the country, the mood of France's Muslims continues to darken.

There are more imams in France than anywhere else in Europe, and many of them preach hatred and violence and all the crazy cant of the cargo cult that fundamentalists have made of their erstwhile-elegant faith. Villepin couldn't chuck them all out of the country. In fact, the famed poet was hard pressed to get rid of any, no matter how nuts they are for terrorism and the lapidation of women. The longest-running case concerned what Le Monde called the "enigma" of the imam of Vénissieux. The enigma, to Le Monde, was how could a man who looked so holy and who even said he "likes women" advocate stoning them as an appropriate form of domestic discipline? It turned out to be easier to take

Brigitte Bardot to court and fine her into silence for pointing out that Muslims are not exactly the best friends of livestock. All that ritual bloodletting made Brigitte's own blood boil.

■ ■ ■ ■ ■

BEFORE SARKO'S TENURE, the figures were really ugly: In 1999, crime in France was rising while in the United States it was falling. By 2001, crime had increased 7.2 percent over the figures for 2000; murder and attempted murder were up 35 percent; sexual assaults increased 40 percent; pickpocketing on the Metro was up 38 percent. In 2002 there were violent clashes in Paris following Le Pen's electoral surprise. On Bastille Day 2002, Chirac survived an assassination attempt. In October 2003, the mayor of Paris, Bertrand Delanoe, was stabbed during an all-night rave he had organized called "Nuit Blanche." A sizable percentage of this can be laid at the feet of fanatical and angry French Muslims.

The Stasi Commission's report came out against this backdrop of violence and racial tension, and at a time when the French concept of laïcité—formulated in a 1905 statute that was meant to resolve a church-state conflict, but failed to do so—was (and is) still being defined. Since at least 1989, when some Muslim girls were expelled from a school in the Paris suburb of Creteil for refusing to take off their scarves, the French have been struggling with problems that come from what happens when an ill-defined concept is fashioned into statutory art, especially one concerning fashion. Often, implementation of secularism has come down to an individual teacher or headmaster, like the poor atheist dad in all those Pagnol stories. That kind of arbitrary enforcement didn't do much for "race relations." (Neither will the recent decision by the government to give French students a more accurate picture of the Holocaust, since previously they weren't being given a picture at all. In a conversation held in the south of France, students were shocked to learn that the Vichy government had collaborated with the Nazis—"we were taught they were neutral and prevented the occupation," one said—and totally disbelieving that the French had rounded up Jews faster than the Nazis could.)

The government hoped that the Stasi report would resolve all these difficult issues by making "aggressive" displays of religious conviction illegal, while still allowing small items of jewelry to be worn. Obviously, that didn't happen. The report has had absolutely no effect on the larger, more difficult issues concerning Islamification, anti-Semitism and French political cowardice. But in France, some cheese is better than no cheese at all. And the French congratulated themselves on putting one more brick in the wall separating religion and the state by institutionalizing the intolerance of religious symbols in French schools. The papers heralded the report as if it were divine writ. *Libération's* headline: *"Les sages disent oui à une loi sur le voile."* ("The wise ones say yes to a law on the veil.") In *Le Monde,* the joyous religious fervor of the secularists was on display, especially in an item written by liberal intellectuals (or whatever passes for such a thing in modern France) expressing their deeply felt belief in the holiness of the secular state—an article of faith as unswallowable as their bizarre Beaujolais fetish—and explaining that only the ideals of the *république* stood between Frenchmen and the barbarism of people with mainstream religious convictions. Americans, for example. Elsewhere, *Le Monde* took a look at the whole headscarf issue and celebrated the noble, "intriguing" uniqueness of the French character—something so ineffable it couldn't actually be named, yet oddly resembling hypocrisy more than anything else.

In 2004, the headscarf ban went into effect. Many people expected Muslim frenzy, but France was saved by those two French journalists kidnapped in Iraq. The result was to drive the Muslim radicals in France into silence, since Muslim moderates joined the rest of the country in demonstrations calling for the release of the victims. Then, hostage journalists in Iraq not withstanding, demonstrations against the headscarf resumed in Paris and else-where immediately.

So the separation of mosque and state is safe in France for the moment. But if you want to buy milk or bread or Beaujolais on a Sunday in Pas de Calais or Provence, you'd better hightail it to a less secular place, because in France, Sunday is the day of rest and the stores are all shut tight. You can look it up on your little French calendar, in which every week begins with the Lord's Day and in which every single day is labeled with the name of a Catholic saint. But no yarmulkes, no "big" crosses, and no scarves allowed. Rainbow-colored gay-pride buttons? Go for it. Pierced belly buttons? Dude!

5.

When I was a child, in the 1950s, I used to sit on the floor under my school desk during civil defense drills wondering what the world would be like after they dropped the Big One. My impression of atomic bomb blasts, shaped by having seen some photos in *Life,* was that they left everything pretty much flattened, so I figured the postwar world would probably be something Gobi-like—big, sandy, dry. I used to try to imagine what kind of creature (other than me and my mom and dad and my friends) could survive such devastation. So I asked David Ralston, who was under the desk next to mine. His father was a doctor, so obviously he would know.

"Cockroaches," he said.

Was he right? It's still a little too early to tell. But there are some analogous circumstances. For example, let's say you took a chunk of real estate the size of a small continent, devastated it with two of the biggest wars in the history of human conflict, then added a couple of massive genocides first by the Soviets, then by the Nazis, a near-total collapse of most social structures, a megadose of intolerant secularism, a decline in educational standards, a flat-line birthrate and a truly impressive brain drain. Now try to imagine what kind of ideas would survive to emerge from the wreckage.

Right. You get nihilism, anti-Semitism and anti-Americanism, the three knee-jerk, irrational sentiments—they fail to rise to the level of actual *ideas*—that inform the modern intellectual life of Europe, all survivors of a war fought against pure evil. In other words, instead of ideas you get cockroaches.

If you want to snap on the light in the greasy Euro-kitchen that nowadays constitutes *altermondialisme,* come to France when the communitarians gather to strike a pose or two. As a college student, I used to smile condescendingly at a history professor who was always mangling his similes. "In France," he once said, "the Renaissance drew peasants to the city like insects to a magnet." I laughed then. But damn if he wasn't right: November 2003 saw the convening in and around Paris of yet another session of the European Social Forum (ESF), a global, transnational conglomerate of well-organized, well-financed, anarchistic anti-globalization groups that issue lots of proclamations, including the one that defines the ESF's octopus of squishy left-wing sentiments as "a plural, diversified, non-confessional, non-governmental and non-party context that, in a decentralized fashion, interrelates organizations and movements engaged in concrete action at levels from the local to the international to build another world" (*sic*—mangled syntax and all, though I bet the "non-party" part is right; these people are *serious*).

One of the leading personalities of the movement is Tariq Ramadan, a Geneva-based writer. Ramadan is the grandson of Hassan al-Banna, the founder of the Muslim Brotherhood, which is like an Islamic version of the IRA. The Brotherhood's typical method of persuasion: terrorizing, threatening or blackmailing moderate Arab governments into abandoning Western-style liberal policies and replacing them with fundamentalist Islamic policies. I was once caught in Khartoum when the government made one of its periodic reintroductions of *shari'a*. Bars were closed. Several rooms at an old hotel in town became the busiest saloons in town.

However, Tariq Ramadan, who advocates the development of a "European" approach for the Continent's fifteen million Muslims and thus qualifies as a "thinker," had been associated with the more moderate Islamic groups in France—at least until he published in advance of the ESF session his "Critique of (New) Communitarian Intellectuals." In it, Ramadan attacked Jewish intellectuals for being too, you know, *Jewish*. This is precisely the same problem that the Muslims in France have with the Jews. Understandably, the document was widely considered to be anti-Semitic, even by the French elite, to whom anti-Semitism is usually invisible.

But Ramadan is a darling of the anti-American neo-left—which includes quite a few American. *Salon* called him "the Muslim Martin Luther," while to *Time* he was a "Spiritual Innovator" and a "thinker"—although one who improves on the Rodin version by looking alarmingly like Moby in an Armani suit.

Ramadan's document pretzel-twisted the conglomerate of left-wing, antiglobalist, anticapitalist, anti-American and, very notably, pro-Palestinian groups who make up the European Social Forum. You could see this humiliating spectacle unfold in the left-wing, antiglobalist, anticapitalist, anti-American and, notably, pro-Palestinian pages of *Libération,* which now routinely embraces the fashionable notion of calling for the establishment of a secular, "binational" state in Israel. That way, anti-Semitism can gain parity with anti-Zionism. The binational model squares perfectly with the French view of Israel, in that it would allow the Jews who live there to be bludgeoned into submission by the pro-Palestinian left while France keeps its hands clean of the stain of anti-Semitism. Too late for that, of course, and besides, the Israelis don't seem to want to cooperate. There was also the problem that Ramadan's paper didn't accuse the Jewish Frenchmen of being too *Israeli,* only too Jewish.

Nevertheless, Ramadan confidently offered his critique to *Le Monde*—but they refused to publish it. Not once, but *five* times. Even *Libération* said *non*. It was finally published on Oumma.com, an Islamic site.

Once the document became public, both papers then covered it as news, while others, such as Belgium's *La Libre* and France's *l'Humanité,* provided additional commentary and coverage of the controversy. *Le Monde's* refusal was especially ironic, and no doubt surprising to Ramadan, since the paper has a long history of trying to dismiss notions of French anti-Semitism, often by attempting to draw a distinction between anti-Semitic terrorism and anti-Zionist terrorism. The politically astute left denounced Ramadan, but without much conviction. Some of them admitted to "soul searching"—a thankless job, no? There were calls for Ramadan to apologize, but carefully, since the antiglobalist movement's newest batch of poster children come from amongst the Palestinians. Dozens of Palestinian groups are among the communitarians of Europe, secure in the knowledge that at any ESF gathering there will be an assumption that one Israeli fence is worth killing all the Jews who can fit into a thousand buses. As Mark Strauss wrote in a recent issue of *Foreign Policy,*

> The consequences of embracing a double standard toward Israel are all too apparent at antiglobalization rallies. In Italy, a member of Milan's Jewish community carrying an Israeli flag at a protest march was beaten by a mob of antiglobalization activists. At Davos, a group of protestors wearing masks of Israeli Prime Minister Ariel Sharon and U.S. Secretary of Defense Donald Rumsfeld (wearing a yellow star) carried a golden calf laden with money. Worldwide, protestors carry signs that compare Sharon to Hitler, while waving Israeli flags where the Star of David has been replaced with the swastika. Such displays portray Israel as the sole perpetrator of violence, ignoring the hundreds of Israelis who have died in suicide bombings and the role of the Palestinian Authority in fomenting the conflict. And equating Israel with the Third Reich is the basest form of Holocaust revisionism, sending the message

that the only "solution" to the Israeli-Palestinian conflict is nothing less than the complete destruction of the Jewish state. . . . The very same antiglobalization movement that prides itself on staging counter-protests against neo-Nazis who crash their rallies links arms with protestors who wave the swastika in the name of Palestinian rights.

So, as it happened, the European Social Forum wound up its carnival of seminars and speeches with Tariq Ramadan in attendance after all. Because of the ideological conflation of anti-Zionism and anti-Semitism, Ramadan is essential to the ESF and the communitarian movement in general—which was why, among all the ESF attendees, Ramadan was the only one allowed to convene an individual press conference, covered with some pleasure by the self-justified French press. (By the summer of 2004, he was complaining in an op-ed piece in the sympathetic *New York Times* that he was being kept out of the United States, where he had snagged a teaching job, for reasons that he just couldn't fathom: "The State Department's reasoning remains a mystery.")

The real problem that the ESF movement was having was that, like the anti-American, anti-Bush demonstrators elsewhere in Europe, they have no ideas to put forward, no alternatives that make any sense. That leaves the left mostly content to feed its appetite for sentimental romanticism (for the sake of the children!) by railing against whatever offends their quasi-religious convictions, whether it's the evils of capitalism, the warmongering of the United States or the holiness that descends with the grace of Chrysostom on gatherings of two or more trees. In the truest, most practical sense, the left is reactionary.

Sometimes, that causes problems for left-wing columnists like the *Guardian*'s hapless George Monbiot, who went to the European Social Forum gathering—only to suffer a blinding, forehead-slapping epiphany:

113

In Paris, some of us tried to tackle this question [of the evils of capitalism] in a session called "life after capitalism." By the end of it, I was as unconvinced by my own answers as I was by everyone else's. While I was speaking, the words died in my mouth, as it struck me with horrible clarity that as long as incentives to cheat exist (and they always will) none of our alternatives could be applied universally without totalitarianism.

Meanwhile, on the other side of Paris, another Jewish school was being destroyed. It's now routine for Chirac to go on TV every time a Jew or two gets beaten or killed or whenever a synagogue gets burned or a Jewish cemetery gets defaced, to lead the fight against that most indelible of French characteristics, while the French press runs stories wondering if it could be possible that anti-Semitism was once again on the rise in France.

Sometimes, as in 2003, Chirac announces a commission and launches it into the rhetorical stratosphere: "When a Jew is attacked, the whole of France is attacked." If Jacques is right—and he would be the first to admit that he is—France is under siege.

At the same time, along the German border thousands of neo-Nazis march to demonstrate their peculiarly tattooed muscle. The fascistic National Front is no friend of Israel, that's for sure. And someplace in this gigantic political claw, caught between Islamic fundamentalists, left-wing anti-Semites and right-wing nuts, are France's Jews, facing a rising tide of hatred and violence. In 2004, Ariel Sharon, the Israeli prime minister, took one look at this confluence of left- and right-wing anti-Semitism and told the Jews of France to "leave immediately," for, he thought, no Jew was safe in modern France. This infuriated the French government. They denied that Jews were unwelcome in France, and to prove it, they banned Sharon from visiting.

Marie Brenner, a wonderful writer and reporter, came to Paris for *Vanity Fair* in 2003 and returned with one of those dispatches that Walter Wells finds so offensive:

The facts were these: Between January and May 2001 there had been more than 300 attacks against Jews. From Marseille to Paris, synagogues had been destroyed, school buses stoned, children assaulted. Yet very few of the incidents had been reported in the French media, which have a distinctly pro-Palestinian tilt. . . . On the afternoon of October 7, 2000, Clément Weill-Raynal, a reporter and legal correspondent for the France 3 television network, was walking through the Place de la République when he saw hundreds of people massed for a demonstration. Paris is the city of demonstrations—there are so many that a caption in *The Economist* once satirized the French love of public display as "Another Day, Another Demo." At first Weill-Raynal tried to ignore the noise, the agitation, and the flags of Hezbollah, Hamas, and certain far-left organizations. "They were shouting, 'Death to the Jews! Kill the Jews! Sharon is a killer!' It was the moment when we had arrived at the point that I was afraid of for many years. The junction of leftists, pro-Palestinians, and Arabs had created a new form of anti-Semitism," Weill-Raynal said. Anti-Semitism in France had been considered a right-wing phenomenon that had fueled the crowds howling "Death to the Jews!" in the streets near L'École Militaire during the Dreyfus Affair in 1895, and seethed through Vichy with the deportation of 76,000 French Jews to the death camps. The new form of anti-Semitism, Weill-Raynal understood, was different: it was coming from the left, part of the movement known in France as *le néo-gauchisme,* and it was connected to the country's socialist politics and the difficulties of assimilating the large French Muslim population. It was camouflaged as anti-Israel politics, but the issue was immense and complex.

The fact is, anti-Semitism, like anti-Americanism, is a growing problem in France, and as Islam spreads across Europe and as Palestinian terrorism becomes inextricably sewn into the patchwork of loony causes that blankets the left, it's becoming harder to ignore. A continent that turned its back on the Jews, castrated its own faith, turned from educating children to giving them vocational training in order to feed the feudal appetites of the state, killed its aristocracy and two generations of its bravest men, now lives in the slime of a peculiarly moronic, vaguely Islamified secularism, where serious religious thought dies, but religious hatred continues to thrive. You would think some sort of lesson would be learned, but apparently not.

In fact, a poll commissioned by the European Union showed that a fairly decisive majority of Europeans think that Israel is a greater threat to peace than North Korea, Iran or even the Great Satan, which would be us. Participants were asked to select the greatest threat to peace from a list of perps, so some apologists for the poll thought the problem might have been in the questions. In fact, a more accurate reading might have been obtained by simply asking Europeans a yes/no question, like, "You really hate Jews, don't you?" It was the multiple-choice thing that threw them off.

But it's worse in France than elsewhere. In *The Return of Anti-Semitism,* Gabriel Schoenfeld noted that the French Interior Ministry admitted that in the first two weeks of April 2002 alone, France saw "nearly 360 crimes against Jews and Jewish institutions." In that single fortnight, according to Schoenfeld,

> Gangs of hooded men descended on Jewish victims and struck them with iron clubs. Buses carrying Jewish schoolchildren were stoned. Cemeteries were desecrated. Synagogues, Jewish schools, student facilities and kosher stores were defaced, battered and firebombed. On April 1, the Or Aviv synagogue in Marseille was burned to the ground, its prayer books and Torah scrolls consumed by flames; it was one of five synagogues in France attacked in that period. A kosher butcher store was sprayed with gunfire in Toulouse. Near Lyons, an Orthodox couple was assaulted and beaten on the street. At a soccer field in Bondy, a suburb of Paris, a band of thugs wearing masks and wielding iron bars, heavy steel balls and strips of barbed wire descended upon a teenage Jewish soccer team and set to work beating its members while chanting "death to the Jews." The goalkeeper, a fifteen-year-old boy, ended up in a hospital, requiring a half-dozen stitches on his head. In the heart of Paris's Jewish district, a young Jewish boy was held

in captivity for two hours, beaten and humiliated before being released.

This inadequate survey of one brief interval is infinitely expandable, for the passage of time has brought new outrages.

Complacent elitists in France and elsewhere shrug this off, pointing out that the increase in anti-Semitism is often tied to events in the Israel/Palestine conflict, as if that excuses this rising horror. This is essentially the same rationale used by the French and the Germans when they were scouring the countryside for Jews and sending them to death camps: the Jews asked for it.

By 2004, incidents of anti-Semitism were setting a record pace; the day that the French celebrated the sixtieth anniversary of the liberation of Paris, a Jewish soup kitchen was burned to the ground by French anti-Semites. The majority of the incidents were indeed attributed to French Muslim thugs to whom burning a synagogue was just another ritual enshrined in their religion of love. This has led to bizarre denials, usually by the French government itself, but often by the European Union as well.

The EU recently decided to look into the cause of the rise in violence against Jews in France and elsewhere. The result was a "special report" on the rise of anti-Semitism by the EU's crack European Monitoring Centre on Racism and Xenophobia. A leaked copy said that crazy Muslims were the culprits, especially in France. So the EU tried to suppress the report because it didn't want to hurt anybody's feelings—unless they were Jews. So the draft was reluctantly released in what the Monitoring Centre said was "preliminary" form. A few months later, in April 2004, the "final" version of the report was released just as the European Parliament was finally admitting that its money was going to bankroll Palestinian terrorists—apparently including the al-Aqsa Martyrs' Brigades, the guys who crammed explosives into the backpack of a kid with Down syndrome and promised him seventy-two virgins in heaven if he would just walk over *there* next to those Israeli border guards and blow himself up. The external affairs commissioner at the time, veteran Yank-basher Chris Patten, was blocking the investigation, as he had for months, because he seemed to be worried about the EU losing influence among Arabs in the Middle East.

One way that influence is maintained by both France and the EU is to diminish anti-Semitism to trivial status. For example, in 2003, Romano Prodi, then president of the European Commission, decided to conduct a "seminar" in anti-Semitism, with himself leading the workshop in denial. Prodi told the participants, mostly Jews, "I do not believe that any organized form of anti-Semitism comparable to the anti-Semitism of the 1930s and 1940s is rampant in Europe today"—but failed to answer the question about how some of the $400 million in taxpayer money sent each year by the European Union to the Palestinian Authority is going into the French bank account of Yasser Arafat's wife, and from there, according to the Israelis, into the hands of terrorists.

So the Monitoring Centre on Racism and Xenophobia's report finally came out in an approved version, which claimed that the perpetrators of anti-Semitism are not frenzied Muslim thugs, but angry white guys. Why are white European males angry at Jews? The Centre says it's because of the injustices inflicted by Israelis on the Palestinians. The French government endorsed the report in a hurry.

A little while later, Nicholas Sarkozy told the French National Assembly that it was the policies pursued by the Socialist government of Lionel Jospin that made Americans think France was anti-Semitic. The quaint folkways of the happy Frenchies (burning synagogues, beating up Jewish kids, defacing cemeteries, betraying Israel, funding Palestinian terrorism) had nothing at all to do with it.

■ ■ ■ ■ ■

UNFORTUNATELY FOR FRANCE and for the European Monitoring Centre on Racism and Xenophobia, the real world has its own assertions. Not surprisingly, according to almost all recent studies, most of the perpetrators of the hundreds of recent anti-Semitic acts in France are in fact the Islamic criminals that most people rightly suspect. In France, there are, after all, at least ten Muslims for every Jew. No wonder the Jews of Israel have been vilified by the government of France so many times that, like Americans, the most hateful things may be said about them in civil discourse with no apparent shame. I have heard allusions to Jewish greed and wickedness so many times in France that I no longer visibly wince—progress of a French kind, I guess.

The nation that prided itself on its vigorous secularism is slowly becoming more and more religious, street corner by street corner, something the proudly rationalist French won't even notice until they take the scaffolding off the minarets in front of Notre Dame Cathedral. The combination of rising tensions in the Middle East, Islamification at home, traditional French anti-Semitism and the newly fashionable antiglobalization movement, with its pro-Palestinian assumptions, makes it likely that such acts will only increase. In France, anti-Semites are like cockroaches in the cupboard. For every one you see, there are zillions more, just waiting for the lights to go out.

When I first wrote about this, I received some interesting comments from readers, including a very perceptive note from Dr. Eli Weinerman, a scholar and historian who is working on a study of left-wing anti-Semitism. Dr. Weinerman noted that "anti-Semitism on the part of the non-Islamic left is not racial, ethnic, or religious, it is rather political. Therefore we see quite a few Jews among its proponents." Historically, he wrote, the same type of anti-Semitism was always present among those on the extreme left, "including even Lenin. The truth is that there always was a very thin line between political anti-Semitism, which rejects Jews with ideas [unacceptable to the left], and 'traditional' anti-Semitism, which hates Jews simply because they are Jews."

Some on the left must be ashamed of this. One of those French Jewish intellectuals whom Tariq Ramadan disliked, for example, was the remarkable Benny Levy, who for much of his life was an atheist and a Marxist. As "Pierre Victor," Levy was among the leaders of the violent student protests in Paris in the 1960s. His revolutionary politics led him to help found *Libération* and then to Jean-Paul Sartre, who, late in his life, collaborated with Levy on a series of interviews published as *Hope Now: The 1980 Interviews.*

The book infuriated the French left because in it Sartre seems to dismiss nihilism and Marxism and embrace a form of messianic Judaism. After Sartre's death, Levy became an Orthodox Talmudic scholar. He died in 2004 in Israel.

6.

THE FAMILY IS NOT AMONG the great institutions of French culture. Children are sent off to public schools where the process of indoctrination begins at the ripe old age of *two*. By the age of seven, they are gone for as long as eleven or twelve hours a day. Despite making parenthood a fairly conceptual enterprise, the government cannot convince French people to have more than one or two children. Have three, and some clerk from the Ministry of Rutting, Swiving, Copulation and Propagation or whatever will give you a free French car! *Mais non!* One kid makes for a fun French family. You can take *la petite grenouille* down to Sergent Major and buy her some charming and expensive clothes, then take her to Villette so the kid can get lost while you puff butts and talk with the other dedicated parents about how rotten the British and the Americans are. One child can really decorate a weekend. It might be tolerable with two, if they're quiet. But *three?* Children and cars both need maintenance, and for many Frenchmen, nurturing is really just not their job.

Neither is caring for the elderly, as the events of the summer of 2003 grimly demonstrated.

That summer was a hot one in France. Summer heat generally makes many Parisians happy, because in August, they leave their large and overpriced tourist attraction and, along with everybody else in the country, they head for the south, where it's even hotter. The August holiday is a treasured national institution, along with most other habitual excuses for not working very hard. Add the thirty-five-hour work week given to an overtaxed nation by a grateful Socialist government, and the month-point-five of paid time off each year, and the endless array of three-day holidays and you have a nation that lives in a more or less permanent state of indolence punctuated by unseemly periods of so-called work, which for many French means going to a government office and saying *"non!"* all day long.

The seriousness with which the French take their August holiday can't be overstated. A friend told an enlightening story: At a Paris cocktail party, a married couple—she was a medical doctor—was discussing the plight of their friends, another married couple, both of whom were MDs. The problem: the impending August holiday and a problematic grandmother who was old and infirm and obviously going to need a lot of help to make it from July all the way to September. What a head-scratcher. However, a precedent from their recent past proved helpful: when the grandfather was suffering from a terminal illness, he had been given medication that ended his suffering by ending his life. That experience had been quite satisfactory for all concerned, with the possible exception of the grandfather. While the grandmother didn't have a terminal illness, she was quite old and quite unable to live her life as she no doubt would wish for it to be lived. Did that equate to a terminal illness? But of course! The situation was resolved, M. and Mme. Médecin got away on time for the August break and *grandmère* got to go to heaven, where she was probably much happier. The woman doctor telling this story thought it was a curious one because the medical couple had sought her ethical advice, and she had none. Her husband was deeply concerned and was dissuaded from going to the police only when he was told that it was too late, the lady was dead, the family was spending a happy August in Provence, and it might be best to just let the whole thing die, like a rickety old grandma, and, as Clintonian Americans like to say, move on.

That decision was made fifteen thousand times during the summer of 2003. July that year had been miserable. On the 28th, Dr. Patrick Pelloux, the president of France's association of ER docs (*médecins urgentistes*), took a look at the long-range forecast, the number of healthcare workers who would be off-duty, the number of doctors and nurses left behind who were restricted by law to working no more than thirty-five hours, and issued a warning, saying that the number of available hospital beds would be reduced by "25 to 30 percent" because of a lack of trained medical personnel. The Chirac government, including the health minister, Jean-François Mattei, disregarded the warning and prepared for their holidays.

Right on time, on August 1, according to an Associated Press timeline, Méteo-France warned of a *canicule*—a heat wave, one that had actually started some time earlier, but something most of France only learned about sitting in traffic jams in their Peugeots on the sweltering roads to the beach. By August 4, the temperature in parts of France had reached 40 degrees Celsius, or over 100 degrees Fahrenheit, and more than three hundred people— almost all of whom were elderly and unattended—had died.

The next day, the blanket of heat covered almost the entire country and by August 7, Paris hospitals were collapsing in chaos under a flood of elderly heat-wave victims who made their way to a hospital—only to find there were no beds, no staff and, throughout France, no air conditioning because it was thought to be wasteful and far too American. Hospital rooms were filling with elderly patients who were left unattended in 120-degree heat.

On August 8 alone, more than a thousand people died. In just four days, the death toll was staggering—and it was clear that officials had no idea how quickly the elderly were dying while their families enjoyed themselves. Nevertheless, l'Assistance publique-hôpitaux de Paris (AP-HP), the network of thirty-nine hospitals and clinics serving the *Franciliens*—the residents of Paris and the surrounding Île-de-France—was put on alert and ordered to increase capacity.

On August 10, Dr. Pelloux, the head of the emergency doctors, issued another warning and chastised his superiors. "At the level of the health ministry," he said, "absolutely nothing is happening. They venture to speak only of 'natural deaths.'" Health minister Jean-François Mattei responded furiously from his vacation getaway, issuing a statement that said, "there is no massive obstruction of emergency [health] services." The death rate, he said, was "comparable to previous years, except in certain facilities and one or two *départements* in the Île-de-France."

That night, Mattei jumped into action and announced the establishment of a toll-free telephone system so elderly people who were dying of heat prostration could get somebody on the line telling them to drink plenty of water. More than 12,000 people called in the first twenty-four hours. The next day, at a meeting to discuss the inability of EDF, the French electrical utility, to deal with the *canicule,* the government urged conservation measures. On August 12, 2,200 people died.

At this point, the actual death toll was more than 10,000. The first secretary of the Socialist Party, François Hollande, issued a statement accusing the govenment of being *passif et inerte* in the face of the catastrophe. Prime Minister Jean-Pierre Raffarin, at his villa in the south of France, held a casual press conference and denounced "partisan politics." As far as the government was concerned, it was business as usual. Meanwhile, jammed funeral homes began turning bodies away and a rather alarming number of corpses began stacking up because nobody was around to identify them.

On August 13, another 2,000 people died, so Mattei interrupted his holiday to investigate. Meanwhile, Raffarin authorized the AP-HP to go to the government's so-called "White Plan," which would allow the hospitals in the region around Paris to recall medical health workers from vacation. Pelloux immediately responded that help was needed everywhere in the country. He said he was "scandalized" by the government's lack of response to what he called a "wholesale slaughter." And for the *Guardian,* as well as for other newspapers, he ridiculed the government's persistent claim that the deaths were due to natural causes. "The health authorities have not appreciated the severity of the situation. . . . Meanwhile, the elderly are dying from the heat."

As Jean-Louis San Marco, director of the National Institute of Prevention and Education for Health, told the *Guardian,* "We are facing a human drama, carnage the like of which doubtless has never been seen in France. Yet the impression given is of radio silence. It makes me want to scream." On the 14th, Mattei announced that 3,000 people had died from the *canicule* so far. In fact, the death toll had already reached 12,000. Chirac's aides reassured the nation that the president of France was "closely following the situation."

On August 15, a cabinet meeting was convened to deal with the disaster. Mattei explained to his colleagues, and the nation, that the reason so many old people had died was because "there are more and more [of them]." Clearly, that situation would soon change. As one health worker told journalist Amelia Gentleman, "We are witnessing the sudden disappearance of an entire generation of people aged over 85." Would Mattei resign? *Jamais,* he said. "I have work to do."

On the 16th, the temperature dropped a bit, so Raffarin played it cool and called for "solidarity, not political debate." Not that there was much debate: The Socialists, after all, were on vacation, too, and the implementation of the thirty-five-hour work week—which meant that even those medical workers on the job could not clock more than thirty-five hours each week, no matter who was dying in the hallways and beds—was their doing. The next day, Mattei told reporters that the situation was "under control" and vilified Pelloux and his claim that the toll had reached 5,000 lives. The daily death rate had eased—now it was merely hundreds a day, not thousands.

On the 17th, Mattei found a culprit—Professor Lucien Aben-haïm, the director-general of public health. Finding a fall guy allowed Mattei to admit that the 5,000 figure was "plausible" after all, while blaming his underling, presumably for not telling him that it was very hot and that there were a zillion old people who had been abandoned by their families. "I am now privately convinced that we did not have the information or the warning signal that we should have had," Mattei told reporters on the 18th. "I feel that as soon as we were alerted, we did what we had to do, but I'm not sure we were alerted soon enough." Abenhaïm immediately resigned, saying he had been made a scapegoat.

On the 19th, Mattei said he thought the whole thing over and found that he had done nothing wrong. On the 20th, Raffarin said the government would try hard to figure out how many people had died, and promised to have official figures within a month. The next day, a tanned and debonair Chirac, who had not bothered to interrupt his vacation or even to express much concern from afar, finally spoke to the nation via television. He promised that the government would make a big, bold plan so that something like the *canicule* catastrophe wouldn't happen again. He also consoled the families of "the many people who had died alone in their homes." Meanwhile, hundreds of bodies were still lying about unclaimed, despite calls for relatives to come forward, including a very well-publicized appeal from the mayor of Paris on the 24th.

On the 26th, Jean-Louis Debré, the leader of the National Assembly, agreed to convene an investigation into the affair. Newspapers in neighboring European states (but not in France, of course) began gently pointing out that it had been hot there, too, but they didn't have massive deaths on their hands. Health ministries and other experts were consulted by the *Guardian*, which came up with this list of heat-wave-related deaths outside France:

- Netherlands: 500–1,000
- Portugal: 1,316
- Spain: 100–500
- Germany: 32
- Italy: perhaps 2,000

A poll was taken to measure the public outrage. Just over half—51 percent—said they thought the government "could have handled the crisis better." In the same poll, however, there was near-unanimous agreement that the government's anti-American policies were perfect. The leader of the Green Party, Gilles Lemaire, approved of the government's lackadaisical attitude, saying it was faithful "to the political culture of liberalism," without explaining how.

It took almost six months before the French government admitted that 15,000 of their most vulnerable citizens had died in the heat wave. The bold, new plan promised by Chirac? The government will buy one single-room air conditioner for every hospital—eventually. And next time there's a *canicule,* the government promised, the elderly will be told to avoid going to the hospital and instead directed to go to a cinema. Maybe they'll get to watch *Some Like It Hot.* Four or five more summers like 2003 and many of the demographic problems confronting France would pretty much be taken care of.

But even God knows when enough is enough. The summer of 2004 was one of the coolest in recent memory.

7.

There are always a bunch of stories in the European press about the ironies of death—its charm, its ability to create empathy, its unique sense of timing. Some of them have made me think of poor Jean-Dominique Bauby.

You may remember him; many certainly do. To me, he's the paradigm of what a Frenchman should be and what so many are. No, not dead. *Heroic*—in a way that is ineffably elegant and profoundly intelligent.

Bauby was the editor in chief of the French edition of *Elle* who suffered a stroke in December 1995 and woke up three weeks later a quadriplegic. His only means of communication was to wink his left eyelid. That, my friends, is an ironic literary device if ever there was one. So he wrote a book—English title: *The Diving Bell and the Butterfly: A Memoir of Life in Death*—blinking it out one letter at a time from his hospital bed.

As he wrote, trapped in a motionless body, he realized that even if all he had to work with was the flutter of an eyelid, "There is so much to do. You can wander off in space or in time, set out for Tierra del Fuego or for King Midas's court. You can visit the woman you love, slide down beside her and stroke her still-sleeping face. You can build castles in Spain, steal the Golden Fleece, discover Atlantis, realize your childhood dreams and adult ambitions."

The book was published in 1997. Two days later, Bauby died. But his astonishing book continues to give cheer to those who face life's ultimately impossible odds.

Bauby lived his last months looking at the ceiling of room 119 in a grand *asile maritime* built in 1869 by Napoleon III's wife, the Empress Eugénie, in Berck-sur-Mer, a chilly and channel-facing fishing village. The empress's new hospital was intended to give care to old fishermen and a few widows of the sea. They certainly needed the shelter; although a home to sailors for much of its history, Berck has never had a safe harbor, at least until they opened the hospital. When they did, the old men and women moved in and spent their days sadly watching younger men empty their nets onto the broad beach below.

Now, the doctor in charge of the institution was a kindly gent, a friend to the town's more creative types. He liked his patients a great deal—admired them, even—and thought it might boost morale a bit to have a painter come in from time to time and make pictures for the amusement of them all. So he persuaded a local artist, the remarkable Francis Tattegrain, to come for a visit, meet some of the old folk and see what he thought might be possible.

Tattegrain took one look at the faces that had been baked for a lifetime in the stiff, salt air, quickly set up his easel and soon began making small portraits of the hospital's elderly inmates, some of whom no doubt lived for a time, then died, in room 119. The result: a remarkable series of canvases, all the same size— small, maybe 6x9 or less—with the name of the sitter and a few notes, such as a nickname or a pithy quotation, scribbled across the top of each. It was a project that took him to the end of his life, in 1915, and beyond: his friend and fellow Berckois, Charles Roussel, picked up and pursued the task until there were ninety-two little portraits, each the same size and scale, now hung in two even rows around three walls of the small closet-sized room dedicated to the collection.

To see them, you have to wander down a passage in the back of the Musée de Berck, a converted gendarme station on a dull street in a grim, down-market beach town overshadowed by its only slightly ritzier coastal neighbor, Le Touquet. These towns on La Manche are resorts for the truly desperate. Coalminers on holiday built Berck's boardwalk, such as it is. Its modern claim to fame is a kite festival. But it's worth finding the pictures. By walking off the street, through the museum and finally into the room, you are treated to an unusual experience: you find yourself the subject of intense scrutiny, with all these salty characters surrounding you with their half-toothed grins, their cartoonlike noses and their dark, lively eyes staring at you like you're a pile of fidgety whiting. On your way out, you nod as you pass another, slightly larger portrait, this one of Victor Ménard, the doctor who was so dedicated to his charges that he arranged to give them a life after death.

■ ■ ■ ■ ■

THAT WAS THEN, AS THEY SAY. The most famous medical man in Berck these days is Frédéric Chaussoy, until recently the doctor in charge of the Berck hospital's intensive care unit. His fame comes from his decision to kill one of his patients, a very unhappy man named Vincent Humbert.

M. Humbert was the victim of a traffic accident that left him a deaf-mute with just one functioning limb and some marginal eyesight. He asked to die and the doctor, who believes in euthanasia regardless of the law, obliged him. When Dr. Chaussoy made his decision, he wasn't acting on whim: Humbert's refusal to live the life of a profoundly crippled man had been featured in the pages of French newspapers for some time—in fact, for a year or so, ever since Humbert had sent a well-publicized letter to Jacques Chirac asking the president to relax the law forbidding euthanasia so he could die "with dignity," to vulgarize a once-fine word.

The story in *Libération* and the other papers gives all the tragic details: unwilling to live after the accident, Humbert begged his mother to kill him. She tried, like many modern mothers would, by pumping a megadose of barbiturates through his IV after granting a series of media interviews explaining in advance her reasoning.

But all this did was put him in a coma—and send him to the Berck hospital. There, Dr. Chaussoy pulled the plug on Vincent Humbert the day before his book—in English, *I Ask the Right to Die*—was to be published.

129

Humbert's book, like Bauby's *The Diving Bell and the Butterfly*, went on to become a French bestseller, although I suspect to a different cohort of readers. The case quickly became a political issue for the left, as all good, high-profile, dramatic episodes do. In this case, the sentimentalizing of the euthanasia "debate" is irresistible to those of a liberal bent. It's highly unlikely that either Humbert's mother or the doctor will ever spend a minute in court.

But the mood in France was spoiled somewhat by the simultaneous reappearance in the press of Christine Malèvre, a nurse who is trying to reverse an earlier court decision that found her guilty of killing her patients (the number is now up to seven) and sentenced her to ten years—despite the fact that she, too, had a book deal (something called *Mes Aveux*—"My Confessions"). Her defense: she only killed patients either by accident or "at their request."

Her embrace of euthanasia was a rather awkwardly timed appeal to public sentiment, coming as it did in the wake of the Humbert affair. The French press has been less inclined to sanctify Malèvre—although she did have a run as the "Madonna of euthanasia," something that might have got her sued if the real Madonna of euthanasia read French papers.

Perhaps the slippery slope blocked the media's view, since the only apparent difference between those who asked the nurse to kill them and Vincent Humbert is that the people whom the nurse killed were terminally ill and not very good at generating publicity or book deals. Or wait! Is somebody saying that a doctor who just happens to be a man is more compassionate than a nurse who just happens to be a woman?

■ ■ ■ ■ ■

BECAUSE EUTHANASIA, LIKE ABORTION, looks fabulous when tarted up to resemble a moral stand, the French adore the idea. In fact, it's an idea whose time has come back from the dead ashes of tyranny's camps. So it's welcome in France—but not so warmly regarded in Germany, where a doctor who just happened to be a woman was arrested in the deaths of seventy-six cancer patients in her clinic. She claimed that all seventy-six were terminally ill. The clinic denied everything. The doctor didn't talk. But the German left was unsuccessful in sentimentalizing the case. Why? Perhaps because Germans have already had some experience with euthanasia. In fact, the story broke as German papers were carrying the news that a new online archive had been established to help relatives anxious to determine whether or not some two hundred thousand missing family members had been victims of Nazi euthanasia programs.

Only three nations in Europe—the Netherlands, Belgium and Switzerland—currently allow euthanasia. Maybe that will change, since euthanasia is increasingly seen as a kind of "right," which makes it perfect for adoption by the European Union. It's the new continental rage. In Italy, for example, a mother cries in the press for the right to kill her suffering daughter, and those who oppose her are heartless. In Spain, a new poll shows that 60 percent of doctors want euthanasia legalized. The European Commission is ready to reopen the debate. Even the local parliament of Guernsey is weighing whether or not islanders should be put out of their misery if life gets too miserable.

But it's in France where euthanasia has become one of the Rights of Man. The idea of mercy killing reflects the modern, secular European ideal, in that it asserts that man's mercy is superior to God's. Maybe one day teleology will finally be stripped of its nasty theological-philosophical taint and made into a medical specialty, like urology. Or maybe European doctors themselves will take the lead. According to one recent German newspaper story, they've started killing *themselves* in the operating rooms. I guess if you're a guy who practices euthanasia, *that's* a mercy killing.

But if you're a guy like Jean-Dominique Bauby, creating beautiful prose out of eye-tics and fighting against death to do so, it's a tragedy, and the kind that could only be ignored in France, where, one year after she successfully had her son killed, Marie Humbert met with the new French health minister and presented him with a proposed law that would make medical homicide a legal act. She suggested naming the law after her son.

8.

When you live in a country where the whole idea of soldiering on is dubious, someone like Jean-Dominique Bauby notwithstanding, eventually a kind of civic ennui sets in. Over the years, voter turnout has been decreasing in France's marginally significant regional elections, and those who do turn up are angry. Not only has Jacques Chirac's party been regularly hammered lately, it has been hammered by a Socialist opposition that is largely leaderless and a National Front party that is largely mindless.

This is part of a pattern. In the last presidential elections, in 2002, the left was so bored and enfeebled by its own litany of fifty-year-old bromides that Lionel Jospin, the Socialist candidate, couldn't even field enough votes to enter a runoff with Chirac. Jean-Marie Le Pen, the perennial National Front candidate, came in second, allowing him the chance to run against Chirac from the right. Enough somnambulant leftists staggered to the polls to allow Chirac to win in a huge landslide.

Two years later, the regional elections showed just how fragile all French governments truly are. The center-right of French politics, the domain of the Gaullists and their ilk, is occupied by a squabbling set of minor parties, including Chirac's unfortunately named Union for the Popular Movement, which was formed by merging his previous party, the Rassemblement pour la République, or, more conveniently, RPR, with some smaller parties. The left is occupied by the Socialists, the Greens and the once powerful but now insignificant Communists, whose sole redoubt is their influence over the CGT, the country's biggest trade union. The National

Front, the bitter and xenophobic party founded by Le Pen in 1972, is on the far right.

After being body-slammed at the polls by Chirac's political opponents, Jean-Pierre Raffarin, the current prime minister, is less important now than ever, and he wasn't very important then. He would already have been completely abandoned by Chirac, no doubt, if the president hadn't been afraid of the alternative—ambitious Nicholas Sarkozy, at this writing the finance minister, but soon, no doubt, the president of Chirac's own party, thus outflanking the Elysée's old crook; for Sarko is the man who would be Jacques. The entire center-right has been mobilized to stop his inevitable triumph. In an effort to suppress the growing cult of Sarkozy, Raffarin told *Le Nouvel Observateur,* "I am the pilot of the Airbus of government." The travel industry should have protested.

In France today, unemployment is high, the economy is flat, there's a growing resentment of the EU and corruption is everywhere. Raffarin has tried to propose reforms to address the first two issues. But, as everybody knows, the French have their little perks—among them, day care forever, a thirty-five-hour work week, employment for life, more vacation than a teachers' union shop steward, subsidies for everything French, a lottery-sized pension and virtually free health care. Raffarin's lame reforms were only a whispered threat to diminish those guarantees modestly, but that was enough to make him despised. His only moment of leadership splendor in the last few years came when a bomb was found on a railway line leading to Switzerland. Raffarin went on TV and told everyone to remain calm. At about the same time, the mysterious terror group AZF sent a letter to the authorities saying they were going to stop planting bombs on the tracks because they were having technical problems, but would resume their work once they'd ironed out the details. In inspiring calm, the AZF, whoever they are, did a much better job than Raffarin.

So poor Raffarin—who came to power as a well-liked, down-to-earth, man-of-the-people kind of fellow—quickly became the most unpopular prime minister in years. Why? Because he's the man Chirac put in front of the effort to implement those desperately needed financial reforms and the French will never be interested in reforming anything until the whole mess comes tumbling down.

The role of the French government is to provide for the needs of the French. That's a pretty broad mandate, but when it isn't met, there's trouble. For instance, when Raffarin's government tried to publish a public health law concerning the tendency of some French people to drink those five-dollar bottles of very excellent Burgundy to excess (I found a bottle of the very rare Gallo red in my local French supermarket; *pas mal!*), vintners were immediately all over the boulevards. The law, complained the purple-footed protestors, was ruining sales. Meanwhile, those hardworking Frenchmen who, in the words of *Sud Ouest*, were *"victimes de l'intransigeance de l'administration Bush"* simply because they cruelly force-fed cute ducks and geese, harvested their enlarged livers, ground them up in what may have been unsanitary conditions and smeared them on toast, were up in liver-spotted arms after the U.S. banned French *foie gras*. The paper claimed that the ban was in retaliation for the French ban on U.S. chickens after the most recent mad-chicken scare or whatever it was. The government's money problems just aren't an issue to voters. They don't care if the government's broke any more than they care about Granny frying away in a heat wave. When it was suggested that maybe a few spending cuts might stave off economic collapse, even the mimes went out on strike.

To mollify voters after the more recent round of regional elections, Chirac accepted Raffarin's resignation, then set about building a new government—by reappointing Raffarin as prime minister. That's the political equivalent of bungee jumping.

The charade fooled nobody; even the French press could see through it. *Le Monde* warned Chirac of the dangers of "scamming the voters." To the editorialist at *Libération,* it was "the end of Chiraquisme."

Not quite. Self-published poet and Napoleon biographer Dominique de Villepin, perhaps the most reviled Frenchman in American history, was moved from the foreign minister's slot to the Interior Ministry, where he set about trying to win the hearts and minds of the angry Muslims who will burn down their squalid suburban ghettos as soon as they can find enough money to buy a match. That may have put Villepin in line to become the next prime minister instead of Sarkozy, at which point the unions will tear him apart—poems, hair, pomposity and all—even if it takes them a (thirty-five-hour) week to do it. The hope of the French government, no matter who's running it, is to just keep France afloat long enough for the country's financial strategy to kick in.

That strategy has the virtue of being quite simple. It's to wait for the American economy to rise high enough to float the French boat. There is no other way of reviving the French economy.

That kind of reliance on the United States doesn't sit well with French politicians, and it never has. Creating a political and military rival to America and isolating it as much as possible from the rest of the world is the fascination that always governs French policy. France's other great hope? The European Union, naturally.

the weapon

ACCORDING TO AN ANTIFRAUD WARNING issued by Eliot Spitzer, the attorney general of New York, a typical con artist's riff runs like this: " 'You can trust me,' says the scamster, 'because I'm just like you. We share the same background and interests. And I can help you make money.' " Smart Europeans can smell something peculiar in the air above Brussels, the capital of the European Union. Maybe they're just savvy consumers.

The entire European Union is a mammoth affinity fraud, where every single national leader talks to other national leaders and says, more or less, "You can trust me, because I'm just like you. We share the same background and interests. And I can help you make money." If that sounds like a flimflam to you and me, it sounds like pillow talk to the leaders of small, insignificant, government-choked countries like France.

As with any affinity fraud, there are a number of polite fictions that must be observed if the scam is going to work. One of them is that France will triumph if it can frame that triumph as the emergence of an anti-America in the form of the EU.

What a bizarre creation that thing is. If there were science fairs for mad political scientists, those who designed the European Union would win the grand prize. Treating each of the nations in Europe like a body part—with Germany as the muscle and France as the brains—and stitching them all together to create a bureaucratic Frankenstein is like the stuff of horror films. The whole thing seems so obviously a fantasist's concoction, it's amazing that it has survived at all.

In the 1960s, when my generation went to college, turned up the stereo, stole all the towels and tore the place apart, liberal arts majors were a favored class. Because science was linked to the military-industrial complex, it was thought unwise to disrupt the delicate, melancholy iambs of our pastoral thoughts with discouraging information concerning rockets and explosives.

Instead, science was offered as a sort of single-sentence statement. One of my college's geology classes—the local lit-major variation of the infamous "rocks for jocks" course—involved piling into a bus and driving through the countryside while a teaching assistant said, "That's quartz, that's granite, let's go home." Anybody along for the ride got a "pass"; if you missed the bus, you got a "fail." Talk about grading on the curves. Once they passed science, they could graduate—and maybe even become educators, the kind of people who would be paid to reform previous educational reforms, adding another circle to the great downward spiral. Thus did a generation of slackers infect the education business with the virus of credentialed lunacy that now has spread through every aspect of academic life.

Speaking extremely literally of academic life, my own adventure in science involved growing mold in a petri dish. I used the dish mostly because my shower curtain was too bulky to bring to class. The idea, I recall, involved establishing a colony of disgusting, unspeakable *stuff* in a warm and friendly environment. Think Malibu.

You started with spores, which I think were small and insignificant. For a while, nothing happened. Then, almost instantly, you had a vast population of fuzzy semi-vegetation that threatened to overwhelm its own little petri planet. It was like growing your own fright wig. The science takeaway: Nothing beats breeding a low-life form so you can make jokes about it later.

Then there's the giant petri dish in Brussels. Europe's boosters like to pretend the spore was taken from the European Steel and Coal Treaty of 1951 and planted in 1957 with the Treaty of Rome, the European Economic Community's birth certificate. In fact, the latest effort to unify Europe has a slightly older pedigree. In addition to De Gaulle's wish for a European military effort to counter American power, Germany has long had an ambition to mount a unified European economic offensive against the United States. In the words of former German finance minister Walther Funk, "The United States must give up the idea of forcing its economic conditions on Germany and Europe."

Funk, as it happens, was Hitler's economist, and one of the principal architects of the so-called "New Order" envisioned by Hitler. He was also the Nazi state minister who in 1938 drew up the laws banning German Jews from engaging in commerce. As early as 1941, Nazi propagandists were proclaiming that "the United States of Europe has at last become a reality." In his excellent and contrarian survey, *Dark Continent: Europe's Twentieth Century,* historian Mark Mazower pointed out that the Europe proposed by Funk and other Nazi strategists "bore more than a passing resemblance to the postwar Common Market. The 'New Order' beloved of the youthful technocrats at the Reich Ministry of Economics involved the economic integration of western Europe and the creation of a tariff-free zone."

The plan advanced by Funk and others saw a common currency, a central bank and the other institutions that are critical to the European Union today—in the words of Hermann Neubacher, described by Mazower as "Hitler's Balkan supremo," a unified "*Grossraum* which instead of individual countries would form the economic unit of the future." From the moment of its inception, the Nazi version of the European Union had the support of France; in fact, it was the Vichy deputy premier, Jacques Benoist-Mechin, who announced that France was ready to "abandon nationalism and take [its] place in the European Community with honour."

Eugen Weber, writing in the *Atlantic* in 2001, observed that for the French as for the Germans, Hitler's New Order was above all *European.*

> With French and German bankers, industrialists, and other businessmen meeting regularly, the idea of a United States of Europe was making its way, along with visions of a single customs zone and a single European currency. The European Union, its attendant bureaucracy, even the euro, all appear to stem from the Berlin-Vichy collaboration. Bureaucratic controls proliferated, administrative and business elites interpenetrated, postwar economic planning took shape—as did that greater Europe in which France's Hitler-allotted role would be one of a bigger Switzerland, "a country of tourism . . . and fashion."

This is not to sully an idea by association; after all, a unified Europe has been attempted many, many times before, and accomplished more than once. Plus, some ideas are just good: I firmly believe that all trains should run on time, for example. But those Germans, they're visionaries. Josef Goebbels, for example, once predicted that "in fifty years' time [Europeans will] no longer think in terms of countries." The French agreed. Sixty years later, Gerhard Schroeder predicted that "National sovereignty will soon prove itself to be a product of the imagination." The French agreed some more. Reading accounts of twentieth-century France, you can't help but notice how little France has been affected by the huge storms that have broken over her. Political personalities come and go, easily moving allegiances from Pétain to De Gaulle. Some suffered as a result. But the placid surface of French political thought has never been seriously disturbed. The worldview of the French elites is the same now as it was in, say, 1933, 1943, 1953, '63, '73, '83 and '93: France has always been far more anti-American than it has ever been anti-German, with the possible exception of the years 1914–18. The bogus claptrap that Chirac mouthed at the sixtieth anniversary of the Normandy invasion about the enduring friendship between the United States and France is getting creepier and creepier with every passing year.

The predictions of Goebbels and Schroeder may not yet have come to pass for the rest of Europe, but they're certainly true for the political leadership of France and Germany. In fact, for France, and lately for the rest of the world, "Europe" has always equaled France + Germany. For the bureaucrats in Brussels, Goebbels and Schroeder are both a little late, but a lot right. The Treaty of Rome, which followed Goebbels' pronouncement by only fifteen years, was supposed to make Italian pasta attractive to grocery shoppers in Luxembourg and German cars affordable to Belgians. Now, after nearly five more decades of festering growth by functionaries feeding on the rich agar of mysterious taxes and near-unaccountability, the old New Order, rechristened the European Union in 1992, has reached maturity as a gigantic, monstrous parasite, a bureaucratic mistletoe under which the French and the Germans force other nations to contribute to the political well-being of two increasingly unpopular leaders—Chirac and Schroeder—or face trouble from Brussels.

1.

The primary political unit of the European Union at the moment is found in the family created by the marriage of France and Germany, and their immediate offspring, gruff Belgium and little Luxembourg. Think Simpsons with two Homers and two Barts.

Chirac and Schroeder's love is timeless, like a man without a watch. Their "friendship" is marked by an almost complete lack of inhibitions and by occasional public displays of affection, the sort of thing that makes everybody else in Europe and America a little uncomfortable, like a same-sex French kiss. Chirac and Schroeder ridicule that reaction, calling it an example of Europhobia. Whatever, nothing brings it on like a little American-induced insecurity in Franco-Germany.

For example, anybody who says that George W. Bush and Colin Powell have caused strife and division on our troubled planet obviously missed the headline in a September 2003 issue of *Le Monde:* "French-German couple reunited in Berlin." Jacques Chirac and Gerhard Schroeder—that would be Chirac in the *monsieur* role, while Schroeder is obviously the *Herr*—were brought together to celebrate a kind of diplomatic remarriage, something the paper, in an excess of *joie d'Oprah,* called a "renewal of bonds." Best of all, it happened just before the United States went back to the United Nations to ask for help.

The Chirac-Schroeder event was by now a familiar staple of French television newscasts, like some sort of bizarre reality show. There's Jacques, with his happy-drunk grin, and Gerhard, the German-next-door, with the tight smile of a nervous twelve-stepper. That September afternoon, they were preparing for a visitor: Tony Blair was going to call on the couple—something that everyone in the news biz hoped would make for some pretty amusing moments. For Blair, it was all work; it's always so awkward in these situations. Whom do you compliment for the decor? Ultimately, you have no recourse but to goodhearted charity. They look happy, and that's what counts. Besides, who knows what makes a happy marriage work? Some say you need good communication; others say it's all about sex. In the case of Jacques and Gerhard, it's about posturing for votes.

Enter Colin Powell, dropping in like a pop bottle sent down from the gods, with another of George W. Bush's wacky requests for UN help in Iraq. Nothing throws the French and the Germans into each others' laps faster than an American climb-down. A few minutes after Powell's request, France reached not very deep into its own experience and suggested that the United States immediately surrender—in this case, by giving Iraq to the UN so that under French leadership what has been done so badly elsewhere in the world could be done even worse in Iraq. Critics, and I'm one, say that Bush's goofy panhandling at the UN was designed to win over all those Europhiles sitting on fences and listening to NPR in marginal congressional districts. Put that together with all the teachers' union votes he'll get by swamping the Department of Education with money and no wonder he assumed that an election was a mere formality.

Anyway, that little family gathering, so similar to all the others, ended with a little gift: In this case, the parting gift for the United States was some vocational training of would-be Iraqi meter maids in Germany! Cash value: $20. In a *New York Times* op-ed seriously free of any apparent significance or specificity, Schroeder, after conferring closely *behind closed doors* with Jacques, held out a limp, cold hand to his American friends.

As with all of these little press gambits, when Schroeder returned to Germany he polled the crowd and decided where his (not Germany's) interests lie. With virulent anti-Americanism rampant in Germany, thanks in great part to Schroeder's government's encouragement, Schroeder always ends up where he started: back in Jacques's lap, where they commiserate about how neither of them has had a significant electoral victory—but many, many setbacks—since that day they stood shoulder to shoulder in the big *pissoir* on the East River and made water on the UN—and made necessary the Coalition invasion—by making a mockery of the Security Council resolutions aimed at Iraq.

The implacable anti-Americanism of France is occasionally made buoyant by these political climate changes. For example, the anti-Americanism of idea-challenged German and French politicians—that would be Schroeder and Chirac—works for men who are much more concerned with their own electorates than with anything else. Both owe their jobs to their ability to exploit the EU and the UN as instruments of multinational anti-Americanism. The grotesque pre-Iraq diplomatic naïveté of Powell and Bush helped too, of course. Luring them to the UN by personal entreaties—from Chirac to Bush and from Villepin to Powell—the French used the conflict over Iraq as a setup to score a big one against Lucifer by betraying the U.S. and making liars of themselves.

Bush and Powell should have understood that beating up on the United States gives cynical politicians like Chirac the ability to co-opt the French left, which continues to flounder, especially since it has now lost the Stars-and-Stripes-burning franchise to the French center-right. And for center-left guys like Germany's Schroeder, the EU has charm because old-fashioned spending programs are political fairy dust, especially during economic downturns—and double-especially when somebody else is going to help pay for them. Plus, Germany is demonstrably superior to the rest of Europe in developing group hatred. Even before Iraq, according to polls, most Germans believed that Americans were "bloodthirsty"—a sentiment fueled by the relentless rhetoric of Schroeder and his radical foreign minister, Joschka Fischer, more or less the same way Hitler and Goebbels fueled anti-Semitism in the 1930s, and for more or less the same reasons.

Looking back on those callow days, it probably all seems like a dream now, when Joschka Fischer and Dom de Villepin got to play at being butch by teasing the big guys on the varsity, knowing that nobody would pound them later out in the parking lot, which is what they deserved. But there's always a payback. For France and Germany, it's called the economy.

■ ■ ■ ■ ■

THE ECONOMY OF THE EUROZONE rests on the solid bedrock of irrational faith. Take, for example, the EU's economic stability pact, an agreement intended to make nations obey the God-given law of the checkbook. But don't take it seriously, because nobody else does.

The idea, insisted upon by the Germans back in the day when there was a German economy, was to make sure that when the euro became a shared currency, all those lazy Spaniards and those pot-toking, euthanizing Dutch wouldn't bankroll their national deficits by sucking up the revenues of countries, like Germany, that actually produced more than they consumed.

But then came the end of the 1990s, when the fortunes of Europe stumbled, and the French began persistently violating the pact. The French explained that they didn't mean to run a huge national debt, but alas, they couldn't help themselves without working harder, which was obviously quite impossible. Naturally, it was Germany who gave them comfort, support and—most importantly—impunity. Year after year, France escaped without penalty. Then in 2003, the Germans, driven to financial looniness by Schroeder's left-wing government, followed suit. Alone together again, the strange bedfellows decided to disregard the pact they had so badly wanted just months earlier—despite the fury of the Spanish, the Austrians, the Dutch and others who had all sacrificed heavily to stay within the pact's guidelines. The Franco-German abrogation of the euro pact not only created a massive crisis for the EU, it also turned the spotlight on the real benefits of the EU to France. Europe was a great way for the French to float their slowly dying economy at the expense of smaller, rule-abiding nations.

France, of course, is the heart and mind of the Eurozone, sending thoughts to places like Germany, where the heavy lifting is done, or to Belgium, where they make excellent chocolate and bizarre laws. But the message sent by France was that the French budget isn't likely to conform to EU rules until at least 2006, if ever.

The news infuriated the EU, which was furious at itself for allowing France to violate something as important as an economic stability treaty on a whim, so, according to *Le Monde,* it did the only right thing: It sued itself.

Nobody should have been surprised. France and Germany are at the "bottom of the queue" when it comes to following the laws they pass in Brussels, with France as the worst offender by a long shot, and Europeans all know it. No wonder a poll showed that most EU residents assumed the bureaucrats in Belgium were corrupt and that governments were guilty of fraud. One possible explanation: A letter to major European dailies from French prime minister Jean-Pierre Raffarin telling other Europeans that no matter what, they can always "trust France." To do what, exactly, wasn't made clear.

The solution, reached in 2004: the euro pact would become a kind of guideline—a hope against hope, with lots of loopholes to avoid penalties. This would allow France and Germany to run deeper and deeper debts until the end of time, or until other nations start doing the same thing—whichever comes first. The German finance minister was delighted: the proposals, he said, were "what I've been calling for all along," especially once he started calling for them. As for the French, they agreed that as long as the pact wasn't binding, they would have no problems meeting its provisions.

2.

The First Law of Spin Dynamics, as every pundit knows, is that given sufficient context, appearance becomes reality. That's how George W. Bush became a compassionate conservative, how John Kerry became a presidential candidate and how the New York Times became the "paper of record."

Nobody understands this law better than the French. Their hope: the appearance of European statehood will actually lead to a European counterweight to America—with France at the wheel, naturally. To create a superstate to rival the United States, a constitution is essential. Only a constitutional apparatus gives sufficient legitimacy to the military and diplomatic efforts that form the central part of France's long-term goals. And only a constitution enshrines the compulsion toward bureaucracy that is the EU's most remarkable feature.

For many centuries, ruling Europe has been an ambition of many men, some of whom have suspicious connections with the history of Gaul. From Caesar through Charlemagne, Napoleon and De Gaulle, those who have come close have generally found it wise to pause for a few moments of grandeur in order to convince the mob. Playing King of the Continent, as all men know, requires paying attention to the business of symbol and myth: Grab the crown out of the bishop's hands and do it yourself. After all, the whole idea of government relies on a kind of communal, practical myth. As Madison and Company knew, to make people really believe—and I mean *believe* with necessary fervor, the way a potential martyr believes—you need to take a monumental vision, wrap it all up in suitably inflated language and serve it up hot. In unveiling new, improved governments, presentation is everything.

The EU constitution was the slow child of bureaucrats. It was revealed to the world in the kind of language normally reserved for the majesty of a building permit, at an event whose defining feature was that it was tremendously embarrassing. There was a problem with the overproduction: Valéry Giscard d'Estaing, the imperious former French president who had overseen the writing of the thing and who saw every precious word through the eyes of a deaf poet, tried to look regal, but really, the "Ode to Joy" bit seemed more like a scene out of *A Clockwork Orange*. As the TV cameras focused on a smiling, bowing Giscard, Eurocrats hygienically practiced a little agro by pummeling the notion of national sovereignty in the background.

It was a Momentous Event, don't you know, like a Eurovision Song Contest without the tasteful dance numbers. Even those in the European press who tried to invest the event with some solemnity seemed fairly disappointed. The *Frankfurter Allgemeine* spoke for many when it gently pointed out that the document seemed to be nothing more than what it obviously was—a dull draft created by a committee of civil servants. Instead of a vision, there were 460 prosaic regulations signifying the ways and means by which even more regulations to augment the existing 80,000 pages of regulations could be forthcoming. The document also set forth the rights of the proposed hyperstate, but didn't standardize the damn wall sockets. Giscard could have called the thing "The Regulations of Man" and got more mileage out of it.

Then came a grand cocktail party in Brussels, held to launch a weekend of arm-twisting, at the end of which it was thought the EU would have a constitution that everybody back home would just love.

To get a good view of this process in action, I sat in a farm-house in France having supper with a good, old-fashioned British socialist, a charming but unreconstructed wobbly who yearned for the grander days of Wilson, Callaghan and Foot, but who, in addition to his day job, now dourly advises the revisionist members of Tony Blair's New Labour cabinet on certain domestic issues. On the radio was the Brussels summit convened to unveil the first draft of Giscard's shiny new EU constitution, a document so marvelous that its mere appearance had elevated Giscard into the Académie française, whose members are called "the immortals"— which is now what Giscard has become.

My companion was appalled, he said, at Blair's apparent lack of concern that the document was going down to defeat. He blamed what he called the "selfishness" of the Poles, who, along with the Spaniards, had refused to give up voting rights in order to appease the Germans.

The problem, he said, was that Leszek Miller, the prime minister of Poland at the time, and the other Polish politicians who had gone to Brussels were "frightened" of the voters back in Warsaw and Wraclow and were thus the spoilers of what should have been a glorious day for Europe. And Blair, he said, should have called them on it—but Blair! He was a coward, too. The British prime minister boasted of winning a few side issues—a little more NATO-friendliness for the EU's new army, for example. But he did little to save the day for the main issue—the constitution. "And now," said my friend, "we see the result. A disaster."

Not quite. The summit, which was supposed to give common agreement to the draft constitution created by a commission headed by Giscard d'Estaing, was only a partial defeat for the thousands of politicians and bureaucrats who had their hopes pinned on its acceptance. But it was a cheering, if perhaps transient, victory for most Europeans, including the vast majority of Britons, and even many French, for whom, as repeated elections and polls have shown since, the EU has lost its mojo. The Europeans have been exposed to Euromania for decades now and have witnessed the rapid growth of the supergovernmental apparatus in Brussels. Bureaucrats, fed sufficient tax money, multiply like bunnies. Many Europeans no longer think that what they see is very cute.

In fact, as it becomes more and more apparent that the European Union wants to do more than facilitate the movement of commerce and labor across national boundaries—goals that most sensible Europeans embrace warmly, since they smack of less governmental interference, not more—the mood toward Brussels is changing. The forgivable assumption most Europeans made was that in adopting the EU, they would be getting better, more efficient government, not just more government. Now they are finally seeing that the EU also seeks to add yet more bureaucracy to a part of the world that is already heavily taxed and bureaucratically over-upholstered, leaving local government to suffer under strata of subregional, regional, national, European and—if the old Europeans have their way and give more power to the UN—global governments. On a continent that understands from experience how mutable and tenacious serfdom can become, the new, improved EU suddenly is becoming something less than modern, something that under the French and German governments has become more cynical, self-serving and grotesque, defining itself since the Iraq war almost entirely as the anti-America. Since the EU represents more government, more bureaucracy, more regulation, it generally enjoys the support of the European left, most of whom think the average voter is too stupid to know what's good for him. Perhaps as a result, an inflatable EU is not a happy sell. According to one poll taken in 2003, most Europeans no longer thought membership in the EU was necessarily a good thing. Most, in fact, thought it was either a bad idea or one that didn't much matter at all. The European elections in June 2004 were seen as a massive rejection of the EU by voters across Europe. Schroeder was buried by the Christian Democrats, who got twice as many votes as his slowly suffocating Socialists. Chirac's party managed to pull a mere 16 percent of the vote.

To Chirac and Schroeder, the voters' disgust with the whole European boondoggle was only more proof that the EU should have damned the unruly masses and moved ahead even more quickly with the master plan to unite Europe by decree into one empire-sized nation—a New Order, something that might somehow save their miserable careers. But the problem, my British socialist dinner companion argued, wasn't the voters' unhappy reaction to a mega-bureaucracy. The problem was the cowardice of politicians who were afraid to make decisions that their countrymen might despise. Asking the citizens of these countries what they want is a mistake, he said. "Voters are stupid. They always vote their prejudices." The European leaders were happiest with no decision at all.

I wondered aloud if maybe getting the consent of the governed before changing who governs them might not be a good idea. But that was obviously a dangerous notion. "For something as complex as the EU, it doesn't make any sense to ask their opinion," my friend said. Who would expect the common man to understand something as heavy-going as the draft constitution? "Besides," he added, passing a platitude across the table, "that's why they elected representatives—to make these decisions for them."

This certainly was very much the sentiment that had guided the creation of the constitution in the first place. As Labour MP Gisela Stuart, at the time Britain's sole representative to the constitutional commission, told the *Daily Telegraph*, "Not once in the 16 months I spent on the convention did representatives question whether deeper integration is what the people of Europe want. The debates focused solely on where we could do more at EU level. Any representative who took issue with the fundamental goal of deeper integration was sidelined."

Stuart's comments, and a rising sentiment that the EU deserved more skepticism than support, caused Blair, if not Chirac, to stumble momentarily in his effort to end-run the electorate and impose the EU by fiat—a partial explanation for his lackadaisical appearance at the summit. Blair, like the others who had gathered in Brussels, may have been keenly aware of his constituents' fading enthusiasm for the EU. But that wasn't the reason why the Polish and Spanish prime ministers deep-sixed the agreement the first time they saw it. In both countries, voters are generally pro-European. They simply refused to accept one more bait-and-switch deal by the French and the Germans.

There are enough European summits to make a whole new Alps. The one held a few years ago in Nice, when the French were taking their turn to preside over the EU, produced a treaty that was designed to prepare the EU for a huge expansion that would see the admission of ten new member states, including Poland, the Baltic nations and others. In a complex formula intended to streamline decision-making in Brussels, Poland and Spain were each granted a weighted vote nearly equal to the weighted votes given to each of the EU's largest states—the UK, Italy, France and Germany.

The Germans have never been very happy with the arrangement. They point out that they have a larger population than the other members and contribute way more money to the EU than others. But the postwar history of European unification is essentially one of French paranoia and German penance, so at Nice, Chirac, with one of those Gallic winks of his that resembles a drunkard's tic, eventually convinced Schroeder. The German went for the deal, with the assumption that it could all be ignored later. Like the EU's economic stability pact, nurtured into existence by the Germans but violated freely by the French, and like the Kyoto Protocol, which the EU knows it won't meet, the Nice treaty, to both Chirac and Schroeder, was one of those rhetorical fictions that by now are routine in the Franco-German manipulation of the EU. In the process of inventing the EU, when actual progress toward unification is not possible, the appearance of momentum toward unification always is, and Chirac apparently felt that a bogus agreement was better than no agreement. So an agreement was made. The Poles, not knowing that the Nice treaty was just pretend, then voted to join the EU based on its provisions.

The new constitution on display in Brussels, however, would have thrown out the Nice treaty and reduced the voting and other perks given to the Poles and the Spanish. The French and the Germans insisted that the Poles play along. But Prime Minister Leszek Miller said no—and rather plainly, too. Within hours of complaining about the American refusal to allow France and Germany to receive U.S. contracts to help rebuild Iraq, Schroeder threatened to withdraw the financial supports that the EU had promised to Poland. Miller left. And on a Saturday night, the party in Brussels broke up. By the following morning, the statesmen of Europe were all back home and in church or someplace.

Blair's diffident, aloof role in all this was easy to explain. Almost all the serious threats to his political survival come from his own left, where Europe is generally adored. His electoral victories have all been over his own left wing; his successes have all come at the expense of their policies and their special interests, and his triumphs at the polls have all been huge. On a wide variety of issues, ranging from the war in Iraq to reforming nationalized health service to proposed fee increases for university students,

Blair is under heavy attack from the old Labour left, for whom the Blairite notion that government is by definition inefficient is anathema and subject to endless criticism in the *Guardian* and other leftist media. The Conservatives, meanwhile, haven't been a serious threat to Labour in years, since it's impossible to be to the right of a British politician who privatizes the *water supply,* for pity's sake. There are only two vulnerable spots on Blair's right side: Taxes are one. Europe is the other. The British are getting angrier and angrier at having Europe pushed past their stiff upper lips and down their throats.

So Blair could stroll through that summit, as he has done at others, make some sorry noises and go home the happier. It's an odd aspect of his character that he can't see the inconsistency in his push for yet more in-your-face EU stuff. He must know that the giant machine in Brussels that churns more and more bureaucracy, regulations, edicts, protocols and commissions has no reverse gear. It can do only what it has been designed to do: create more and more government. But Blair is a left-wing politician, for whom there's no such thing as too much government—provided it's left-wing government.

For Chirac (and for Schroeder), episodes like the Brussels constitutional pageant came with a need for a much higher pay-off. Britain's economy actually works. Although stuffed full of government garbage, Britain has an economic climate that does go through warm periods. Germany and France live in perpetual winter. With their huge pensions, their aging populations, and their unrelenting bribery of voters, there is no spring thaw in sight for either of them, unless the heat generated by Wall Street and, to a lesser extent, by the FTSE is sufficient to breathe a little life, however temporarily, into the cold, frozen heart of the European Union.

Anyway, the EU constitution is like The Thing. It will become whatever it needs to become in order to survive. So, in the face of growing voter discontent with the EU generally, Giscard's constitution was lightly amended; the Spanish apologized for their national testicularity; the Poles blinked; and at the end of June 2004 the constitution took on a final form and the show will pass to the growing number of states who have decided to allow their citizens to actually vote on whether or not to surrender national sovereignty to a huge bureaucracy and to one of the most corrupt, self-aggrandizing legislatures in the modern world. Any rejection by any of those nations will mean just another no doubt temporary setback for France's grand mission. Making more government is not just a lifestyle choice; it's a way of life. The rate of recidivism among Europhiliacs is 100 percent.

This all matters to us because most Americans, including those in the current administration, see Europe in benign terms. We envision a strong, collaborative partner who will help us defeat those who threaten us. That's not how the French see the relationship between the European Union and the United States at all. The EU superstate, guided by France and joined by a rabidly anti-American Germany, is the heavy weapon in their war against the U.S. The only thing that can stop its deployment will be the increasingly cranky people who will have to live in it and pay for it.

3.

Those who dream that the European Union might become a counterweight to the U.S. should continue slumbering. Impressive though the EU's enlargement has been, the reality is that demography likely condemns it to decline in international influence. With fertility rates dropping and life expectancies rising, European societies may, within less than 50 years, display median ages in the upper 40s. Indeed, "Old Europe" will soon be truly old. By 2050, one in every three Italians, Spaniards and Greeks will be 65 or over, even allowing for immigration. Europeans therefore face an agonizing choice between "Americanizing" their economies, i.e., opening their borders to much more immigration, with the cultural changes that would entail, or transforming their union into a fortified retirement community.

—Niall Ferguson in the *Wall Street Journal*

THE EUROPEAN UNION IS A FABULOUS WAY to move goods, services, money and labor across various national borders. But the survival of France's self-image as a global power, a project that is the single most consistent policy shared by France's elites both right and left, is dependent on their ability to draw together Germany, Britain, Italy and the other nations of Europe into a political unit that stands in opposition to the United States, lending reality to the premise of Chirac's famous dream of multipolarity.

For most of 2003, the French pressed forward with their plans for a unified European military, something they said would have been "useful" in expressing their point of view regarding Iraq. Meaning what? That they would have put troops between the United States and Saddam? Funny, no? For the last fifty years or so, we have been laughing off European military potential. In the calming stereotypes we all enjoy, France is a nation of short cowards and Germany is a nation of goose-stepping morons. But pause for a moment and think of what French politicians could do with an army of Germans.

Thanks to the British, the current climate won't allow for a lot of EU army-making at the expense of NATO. The current example of the EU-led force in Bunia, Congo, isn't very inspiring. Nobody has the money anyway, and the sudden expansion of the EU has made France a little smaller than it was this time last year. For several months before they joined the EU, Chirac had been agitating against the United States by holding the EU club over the baby seals of Eastern Europe. Said Hungary's prime minister, Peter Medgyessy, who was among those accused by Chirac of being "badly brought up" for endorsing the American position on Iraq, "The greatest lesson I learnt in the last ten months was the lack of dialogue, which led us to different opinions regarding Iraq and other issues. I would like Europe to acknowledge that a Europe of 25 countries will require much more intensive dialogue." Jump back, Jacques! Seals bite! And despite the fact that anti-Americanism has reached pop-culture status in the UK, the British aren't likely to change their minds soon. One recent Mori poll showed that 55 percent of British respondents consider France to be Britain's least reliable ally, while 73 percent think the United States is the country's most reliable friend.

At the same time, as the *Washington Post*'s Jim Hoagland wrote recently, France is getting weaker by the moment:

> For nearly a decade, French policy toward Europe and the world has been dominated by an unspoken conclusion, one that is unspeakable for French leaders and that they exert great energy to obscure. The unuttered notion holds that France is playing a constantly weakening hand in Europe and thus in global politics—and knows it.
>
> The concept of weakness as the center of French policy runs counter to French rhetoric and to a popular view in official Washington and U.S. public opinion. This U.S.-centric view holds that in a paroxysm of Gaullist illogic and self-delusion, France ruthlessly seeks to mold and dominate the European Union and turn it into a global counterweight to the United States, first of all by destroying NATO.
>
> I can't swear that the idea would be totally unappealing to President Jacques Chirac and other French citizens if they thought they could achieve it.

Hoagland's belief is that we've just misunderstood France's desire to placate the Muslims so their immigrant population won't destroy the country while the rest of the world battles Islamic terrorism. Cowardice? It's doubtful, however, that any French politician would ever cop to such a humiliating, but oh-so-French, motive.

If the European Union won't be manipulated to create a hyperpower for France to use against the United States, what's left? The rest of the world, of course. For many years, a favorite French foreign policy objective called *Eurasianisme* has been gaining currency as a way to create a vast interdependent alliance of nations who lack any coherent unifying factor except their hostility toward the United States. By creating a strong and effective European

Union, this reasoning goes, and joining forces with Russia and China, France would finally have the makings of a muscle that could smash its American nemesis. Unfortunately for France, the odds of getting the Russian and the Chinese armies to march to the tune of "La Marseillaise" are long—although the French navy did join up with the Chinese navy in 2003 to exercise their squadrons in the sea off Taiwan, which the U.S. has promised to protect.

Nevertheless, Jacques Chirac spent part of 2004 in Hanoi explaining how much he loved Vietnamese movies because they weren't American, and warning that unless American culture can be defeated, the result will be a "catastrophe." Then he went on to China, where he told the comrades there that France was China's "natural ally." Desperate to sell weapons to China, Chirac flew in the face of existing EU agreements and U.S. policy, claiming the restrictions on weapons sales to China were a "circumstantial measure which is purely and simply hostile to China." Chirac added that there was no justification for the embargo. Not counting those details in Tiananmen Square and Tibet and other places that aren't on a French map.

The Eurasian pipe dream isn't unique to France. You can assume that anything France can come up with as a foreign policy objective has already been well chewed by the American left. In 1997, Jimmy Carter's national security advisor, Zbigniew Brzezinski, described in *Foreign Affairs* a way for the United States to join the grand Franco-Asian alliance instead of fighting it. In "practical terms," it would be a snap:

> In practical terms, all this will eventually require America's accommodation to a shared leadership in NATO, greater acceptance of France's concerns over a European role in Africa and the Middle East, and continued support for the European Union's eastward expansion even as the EU becomes politically and economically more assertive. A transatlantic free trade agreement, already advocated by a number of Western leaders, could mitigate the risk of a growing economic rivalry between the EU and the United States.

The EU's progressive success in burying centuries-old European antagonisms would be one worth a gradual diminution in America's role as Europe's arbitrator.... Defining the substance and institutionalizing the form of a trans-Eurasian security system could become the major architectural initiative of the next century. The core of the new transcontinental security framework could be a standing committee composed of the major Eurasian powers, with America, Europe, China, Japan, a confederated Russia, and India collectively addressing critical issues for Eurasia's stability. The emergence of such a transcontinental system could gradually relieve America of some of its burdens, while perpetuating beyond a generation its decisive role as Eurasia's arbitrator. Geostrategic success in that venture would be a fitting legacy to America's role as the first and only global superpower.

So in "practical terms," all that is required is American capitulation. An interesting scenario: America behaves like a European queen, surrendering power for influence and thereby gaining a generation or so of hegemony. But how did France get into the picture?

They elbowed their way in, no doubt, and nobody bothered to call them on it. It's the French way. Be little, act big. French hostility and animosity are a constant; the French, it turns out, make much better haters than lovers. And as long as France is ruled by an elite clique of corrupt men and women to whom personal profit at the expense of the state is an entitlement, that won't change. In America, it's anybody's guess who will be president in twenty years. It could be anyone—you, your local school superintendent, Chelsea Clinton, anybody but Bono. The American future is anyone's game because it's everybody's game.

But in twenty years, if the citizens of the Fifth Republic haven't revolted by then, or if the nation hasn't surrendered itself to its imams and been repurposed as a faux Turkey—another "secular" state containing millions of true-believing Muslims now anxious to become citizens of the EU—the president of France will be an *énarque,* educated to rule others, trained to pilfer funds, protect his friends and placate those beneath him by promising them what neither he nor they nor their children can really afford. And he'll hate America—but he'll always have Michael Moore.

4.

> Because of all the things that connect us, I'm concerned about the campaigns against my country, and the recent surge of "French-bashing." There's a paradox here, since France is actually among your best friends in the fight against terrorism. . . . More generally, I'm concerned to see both Americans and Europeans expressing doubts over the future of transatlantic relations, and I'm troubled to see that Europe is misunderstood, if not scorned, in the U.S. The European Union is changing. It has opened to the East. Soon, I hope, it will have a Constitution that will make its institutions more effective and legitimate. It is in America's interest that Europe asserts itself as a powerful, reliable partner.
> —French foreign minister Michel Barnier,
> the week after the 2004 election, in the *Wall Street Journal*

MY FRIEND WHOM I'LL CALL JOHN because that's his name had the world's worst marriage. His wife had drug and alcohol problems and, as a result, fidelity and financial problems to boot. After putting up with (read: enabling) her life of crime for two decades or so, he finally told her to take a hike. She spent the next ten years suing him, harassing him, stalking him and threatening him. He kept telling her, directly and through various lawyers and police officers, to stop. She kept asking him why he was so hostile.

France is like the ex-wife from hell. Yes, we enjoyed each other's company once for a couple of months several hundred years ago, but it's over, way over, over and dead, over and over again.

So along comes the foreign minister of France the week after the American electorate made a deliberate decision to vote against a candidate who based virtually his entire foreign policy goals on appeasing France enough to enable France to soak even more concessions from America in exchange for granting a very, very modest gesture of assistance in Iraq. One thousand French soldiers in Iraq would not make a difference unless they all came to serve as body armor for Americans.

It isn't "Europe" who is scorned in the U.S.A. It's France, and "scorned" is too gentle a word. When Americans think of France— admittedly, not often—it's as the punchline in a joke from the Simpsons. Yet only a French foreign minister would cap a couple of years of sabotaging American foreign policy, running up a tab that can be calculated in American lives and treasure and undermining international institutions by writing an open letter to America lecturing and scolding us about our behavior toward his underhanded, duplicitous, insignificant little country with its pretty but largely useless language. The "paradox" is that France thinks it has "best of friends" anywhere on the planet, except this year in Germany. Next year, all bets are off.

The French betrayal of the United States is not a policy, not a strategy, not a political lifestyle. For the French government, including politicians like Barnier, it's a way of life. Like all of France's little caesars, Barnier is a lifelong government employee, a graduate of one of France's *grandes écoles*—in his case l'École supérieure de commerce de Paris—who, according to the *Times* (U.K.), neither speaks nor writes English. What he knows about America, he's learned from watching badly dubbed TV shows on TeleFrance 1.

This is your life, Michel Barnier, from age twenty-two:

■ 1973–1978: Private Office of the Ministers for the Environment, Youth and Sport, and for Trade and Craft Industries

■ 1973–1999: Departmental councilor for Savoie, canton of Bourg-Saint-Maurice

■ 1978–1993: Member of the National Assembly (RPR) for Savoie, 2nd constituency (Albertville)

■ 1982–1999: Chairman of the Departmental Council of Savoie

■ 1987–1992: Co-President, Organizing Committee for the XVIth Olympic Games, Albertville and Savoie

■ 1993–1995: Minister of the Environment

■ 1995–1997: Minister of State for European Affairs

■ 1997–1999: Senator for Savoie

■ 1997–1999: Chairman of the French Association of the Council of European Municipalities and Regions

■ 1998–1999: President of the Senate Delegation for the European Union

■ September 1999: Member of the European Commission, Regional Policy

Barnier is a functionary. As a foreign minister, he is perhaps not as good a poet as the self-published Dominique de Villepin. He is as disconnected from the needs and problems of his own people as the rest of France's ruling clique. His political patron is the president of France, a man whose family defrauded the taxpayers of Paris out of some $3 million. His life, he has said, is wrapped around his "political commitment" to building a European counterweight to the United States. And setting aside the obvious examples of disingenuousness ("France is actually among your best friends in the fight against terrorism . . .") in his open letter to America, it's frankly bizarre for a French foreign minister to talk to Americans about their distrust of France without revealing any awareness of France's own behavior. Barnier's nonsense is merely the first in what will be a long sequence of post-election appeals to an American public that made its decision about France when it made its decision about John Kerry.

Americans know it's not for the United States to worry about a "campaign" against France—and little books like this are hardly a campaign in any case. It's for France to change its ways, not just temporarily to meet the requirements of whatever debacle Paris is confronting, but permanently. If France wants to be seen as a "reliable partner," it needs to align its long-term goals with those of the country it so tirelessly and ridiculously calls an "ally."

Barnier, Chirac and their ilk are the barflies drinking on your tab. They need to realize that every demand they make on the United States comes at American expense. Americans understand that such is the dilemma of the world's sole superpower and all that. But even in sensible American homes, unless there's a drinking problem, charity stops somewhere short of ruin. France should not expect America to be anti-American in order to be an "ally" of France. It's past time for France to be taught that American loyalty is not an entitlement, and that France cannot wage a war on America and expect America to help fight it so France won't get hurt.

I was once a college teacher, and as those who teach know, the politics of the English department are more ruthless and cutthroat than the politics of the real world. Once, while trying to help a friend with five kids and a pregnant wife keep his job, I was forced to realize that the guy I was trying to help was working behind my back to get me fired so he could take *my* job. I didn't know if I should go after the guy or what. So I turned to my own mentor, an old Joycean Jew from the Bronx, and asked him what he thought I should do. He told me to forget it. "His punishment," he promised, "will be his life." And so it has been, to this very day.

It would be nice if the French people—not all of whom, after all, dislike America (remember that 5 percent!)—would suddenly grow up, toss their ruling convicts in jail and start working hard to succeed. But it isn't likely. France's punishment for a history of deceit and treachery is to be France, a shrinking power which in this century will be submerged and ultimately defeated by its own history and politics. In fact, if you look closely at France, the European Union and France's big Arab gamble, you can see that France, true to form, has surrendered already.